BREAK FREE
TO STAND IN YOUR
POWER

COMPILED BY

SEEMA GIRI

AWARD WINNING AUTHOR

Published 2020

Printed in the United States of America

Print ISBN: 978-1-7350255-0-6

Publisher Information:

Uplyft Media

CONTENTS

Section 4: Step Into Your Power

FOREWORD

BY LINDA PATTEN

What does it take to bring together authors with this much heart? What does it take to create a compilation with this much beauty and soul? When an author is drawn to bring a compilation to life, she begins with her own story. She then calls on authors whose stories will resonate with the spirit and purpose of the compilation.

It takes a compiler who has been on the same journey that her authors have been on, who has gone through the trials of a difficult life to come through shining brightly. Seema Giri embodies this journey, having herself broken free from debilitating chronic pain which no one could seem to diagnose or treat adequately, kept her bedridden for long periods of time, and even prevented her from feeling strong enough to hold her own baby. Yet she persevered, advocating for herself and never giving up the fight of her life – for her life and that of her family.

Now, Seema's life work is to help others "break free from overwhelm, confusion, limiting beliefs or chronic pain" that might be holding them back from living the life they are meant to live. *Break Free to Stand in Your Power* is one important way she is spreading this message, by giving healing voice to the authors who have stepped up to contribute to this book – and by sharing with you, the Reader, their personal stories to enable you to get creative with your own path to greatness.

What will you find here? We all have our stories of heartbreak, living on the dark side, and wishing life could be different. In this book, each compilation has a different voice and spirit. The Reader will get wonderful perspectives on how to solve life's most challenging problems from men and women of varied cultural backgrounds, professions, ages, and life experiences. You will realize you are not alone in your own journey, as others have gone through similar situations and come out the other side with great courage, compassion, passion – and hope.

This book is one to be read as the spirit moves you. What do you need to hear today? Do you need a story of courage, of pathos, of redemption? Choose a chapter and see what unfolds. You will find just what you need in the pages of this book.

A note about these authors who have opened their hearts to you, the Reader... Having been a contributing author to seven very different compilations, I have a deep understanding of what an individual is feeling when they say "yes" to becoming a contributor to an anthology. Questions, and sometimes some deep inner reflection, arise: What is the spirit and purpose of this book? Do I have a story to tell that will have meaning to the reader? Do I have wisdom and advice that's valuable to pass on?

It can be very difficult to decide which aspect of their life or stories to share. There are stories in my life that I have been happy to share and inspire; there are others I still find painful to put into words on a page. I believe most authors have asked themselves this question: Do I want to share "that" story? Yet, they look into their hearts, allow themselves to be vulnerable, and courageously choose to tell a story from their lives that will serve others — lessons they've learned that may bring resolution to a painful situation, provide hope for someone in the throes of grief or despair, or show a path to a better way to live.

For Seema Giri, this book is a labor of love. Wanting to get her message out about breaking free to stand in your power, to share encouragement along with tips and insights to raise up the reader to a more powerful level, Seema has found authors to give us hope around mindset and challenges in life and in health. To be "real and raw" takes courage. I commend all of the authors in this book for being just that. Their stories have pathos, compassion, empathy, and joy.

You'll find stories of struggling in high school battling depression and anxiety, overcoming life challenges from arriving to a new home in the United States, taking a courageous step to "choose to be fearless," learning lessons in life and business as a young Girl Scout, experiencing a profound awakening out of a "messy, painful, liberating and brilliantly life-altering" single moment in time, and many more.

As a leadership expert with a similar experience, I am drawn to Seema Giri's own journey to become a successful entrepreneur, coaching thousands of people...yet seeing herself only in the position of supporter, never the leader. She has learned to embrace her power and accept herself as a leader and influencer. Bringing together these 17 inspiring authors for this book (which is a project also not for the faint of heart) is a sterling example of how she is owning her leadership role.

I thank Seema for having the courage to step into this project with such heart and giving us this gem of a book.

A loud and clear message comes from each chapter in *Break Free to Stand in Your Power*: That no matter where you have been, where you come from, or what your past has been, you can make your life's journey filled with more joy, grace, and power. You can, as Seema Giri often tells us, "Rebound, Reset, and Realign your life to embrace your brilliance." This inspiring book is an invitation to all of us to stop sitting on the sidelines of our lives and to BREAK FREE – step up, accept, take ownership of ourselves...and stand in our power.

~~ Linda F. Patten, Leadership Trainer for Women Entrepreneurs and Changemakers – President & CEO, Dare2Lead With Linda

Website: www.dare2leadwithlinda.com,
email: linda@dare2leadwithlinda.com
https://www.facebook.com/dare2leadwithlinda
https://www.linkedin.com/in/lindapatten
http://www.youtube.com/c/LindaPatten

WHAT PEOPLE ARE SAYING...

"Cause your spirits to soar to greater heights and help you achieve your full potential."

-Dr. Sanjiv Chopra
Professor of Medicine, Harvard Medical School

"Enlighten, inspire and motivate you to embrace your own unlimited potential."

-Heather Burgett
Award-winning publicist and CEO/founder of The Burgett Group, Inc

"Give yourself a gift and soak up the profound words in this book."

-Carol Fitzgerald, Author of 6 books & Health Care Advocate

"I would recommend this book to anyone who is going through a tough time or wanting to change the direction of their life."

-Elizabeth Clamon, COO, The Clamon Group

"It will be a cherished instrument toward helping many to journey to their rightful place of power!"

-Nancy Tarr Hart, PhD

ACKNOWLEDGMENTS

"There is no such thing as a self-made man.
You will reach your goals only with the help of others."
George Shinn

I would like to take this opportunity to give thanks to an amazing group of people.

To my husband, Upendra, and children, Aman and Ashima: I'm so grateful for how you have supported me in discovering my new passions. Even I didn't know writing an anthology would be part of my path. You have shown immense love, trust, and compassion. I love you for the way you always cheer me on and encourage me to embrace my brilliance.

I would like to thank Rebecca Hall Gruyter from RHG Media Productions and her team in compiling the various parts of the book into a beautiful masterpiece.

It has been an honor and privilege to work with this amazing group of experts and co-authors. I am in gratitude that they entrusted me to bring forward and share their powerful stories of breaking free to empowerment where they can shine their brilliance and illuminate others' lives to *Break Free* to stand in *their* power!

HOW TO USE THIS BOOK

This book is an excellent and powerful resource for you to help you break free from your challenges or barriers holding you back from the way you want to live your life. The following are some tips and suggestions on how to get the most out of this book and experience transformation.

1. You will need your favorite journal, favorite pen, and a quiet place where you won't get disturbed.
2. In your journal, you want to capture your current state: your fears, frustrations, and where you feel you are holding yourself back or being held back. Be as detailed as you can. This is for your eyes only.
3. First read through *all* the chapters.
4. Go to the chapter you resonated with the most and follow the tips given in that chapter. Use your journal to capture your thoughts and feelings.
5. Go to the second chapter that you resonated with and follow the tips given in that chapter. Continue doing so with the other chapters until you feel complete.
6. Review your journal. Go back over the pages, and you will gain new awareness and a new perspective of your challenges. You will notice your strengths. Perhaps you will even notice a pattern. Once you have this new insight, you will know exactly where you need to make some changes or adjustments to your life. Most importantly, you will see how far you have come in your healing journey.

As you go through this process, you will realize, as you move through your healing journey, you will resonate with the different authors' stories and tips.

Don't forget to celebrate your small wins along with the big wins!

SECTION 1:

Discover Your Power

FEARLESS
BY AMANDA YEARY-TIRAVANTI, ND

Imagine you have attained every goal you've ever set for yourself. I sought an office temp position at seventeen—even when most people wouldn't consider hiring you before the age of eighteen—was hired, and worked ragged. I decided to get a degree to prove to hiring officials and industry professionals that I do know what I know. I graduated with honors and created a career in a male-dominated field of IT networking. I was a well-respected and valued member of the team. Then one night it all fell apart!

I am woken out of a sound sleep. I can't breathe without pain. I can't straighten up without pain. I can't curl into the fetal position without pain. While fighting to breathe, I know that my dinner is going to come up or out. Mind you, I already can't move or breathe without difficulty. I slide off the bed into the floor, knowing there is no way I can walk. I crawl slowly to the bathroom.

After everything came out, I laid down with my back on the cold floor, gently rocking slightly side to side, as the pain slowly subsided, until eventually I was able to slide into sleep. When I woke frozen some time later, I very carefully, to keep the pain at bay, crawled to the kitchen. I got my ice pack out of the freezer and a pain pill out of the cabinet.

The little pill, it turns out, had caused all of this. See, a few days before, my mother had called me, I thought to schedule a lunch date. Instead it was to inform me that a medication I was taking had been recalled because of its addictive properties. She had called to ask me to consider tapering it off. I told her, "No problem. I've never been addicted to anything and I am not going to start now." Instead of tapering I quit cold turkey, and my body revolted.

So, the morning after, she called me with that sixth sense moms have, and asked if I was okay. I recalled all that had happened. She brought me herbs and knowledge passed through generations in our family. She also requested I talk with her chiropractor. To the point of saying, "If I make you an appointment, will you go?"

The chiropractor was able to work me in the following week. His first question was, "Why are you here?"

My automatic response was, "Because my mom is afraid I'm going to get addicted to pain medications."

He was shocked, but it doesn't serve either of us to beat around the bush. After a full exam with x-rays, the diagnosis was Level IV Degeneration Scoliosis. His words were, "I thought I'd made a mistake in looking at your x-rays; they look like those of someone in their mid-forties."

My automatic response: "Well what can I say, Dr. Long? I've always been an overachiever."

While we were both able to share a laugh, the prognosis was grim. I asked, "How do we 'fix' this?"

And the response was, "We don't. There is no precedence for reversal of this severe a case. At best, *if* you do all I suggest, then we should be able to keep it from getting worse."

"Okay. What do you suggest?"

I went home that day disheartened and scared. I was thinking my whole life had just changed in what felt like two seconds flat. I am confronting that I am an addict. I was not to the point that I am not willing to fight the addiction and remove the drugs, but still my body had become addicted to it, which was overwhelming to me. *Then* you add the fact that everything I had ever hoped to achieve just got thrown by the wayside. How was I going to amount to anything? What did I do wrong to be made completely worthless?

I started to look at some of my thoughts. Worthless? Look what I had done. I had competed and made a name for myself in a male-dominated field. Am I really going to give that up? What are my options? Disability? What will that pay? How will I make ends meet with that? What about the traveling I wanted to do? What about the life I wanted to build? I have to throw it all away? For what?

No. I *refuse* to buy that. I have come too far to quit now. I have done too much to throw it all away. I do not agree that there is *nothing* I can do. I will do the exercises Dr. Long gave me. I will work with the herbs like mom and I discussed. *And* I will prove him wrong. I am not disabled. I do not accept that label, and I will find a way to prove it wrong! I will *not* accept the prognosis of "no hope just cope."

Now, did I know how I was going to move forward from this, or where the actual answers were? No, I didn't, but I knew I didn't want the picture they were painting for me. So, the first *true* step to take, to get the most of your healing journey is to become very aware of what it is you don't want, so that you can take the *action* of defining what you *do* want. Truly take the time to envision what exactly you want it will shortcut your journey.

What if you don't know what you want in the end for your vision of what you do want? Does that mean it won't shortcut your journey if all you can see is your next step? No, it doesn't, *but* it will be a longer journey. I know, because it was true for mine. So it is worth it to take that time to truly allow yourself to think *big*, beyond your wildest imaginations, just because you don't know how doesn't mean it can't happen. *But* you have to know where you want to get to before you can ever walk a single step in the right direction.

To help you discover your *big vision*, ask these questions:

- What if the doctors or experts are wrong?
- What if I could have the life of my dreams? What would that look like?
- Does this vision align with your core values?
- Does your vision give you life? (Does it fill you with hope? When you imagine it achieved, does it fill you with life?)
- Will this vision make you grow? (Is it something you already know how to achieve? If so, then it's not big enough. Be willing to think even bigger!)
- Does this vision have some good for others? (If your vision is to attain improved health, you are able to enjoy more time with friends and family—this would be good for others.)

The number one key to success in healing is emotions. That's right I said it: the big E-word. There is a good deal of science to this. It turns out that there was a study done that followed participants from childhood into adulthood. It evaluated people for the number of ACEs they had—Adverse Childhood Experiences. It turns out that the number of ACEs a person experienced was directly correlated to the number and/or types of health issues, such as autoimmune disease, anxiety, depression, and other painful conditions.

The biggest thing with ACEs is that children learn to deal with the emotions of the experience in different ways. They could bury it, ignore it, cope with it, or try to work through it. In this study working through it rarely happened. If no one else has ever said it, let me say it: there is *no* shame in attaining professional therapy, and especially in severe cases. Patience is not a commodity I possess. That being said, I have taken the *long* road. Take me at face value when I tell you: you do not have to repeat my mistakes. Getting the right kind of help is one way to shorten your road.

There are some questions you can ask to self-evaluate the role your emotions play:

- If you are someone experiencing pain, does it flare or become worse in certain situations? If so, what emotions are you experiencing when this happens?

- Do you notice when experiencing emotions that there is pain or discomfort in your body? If so, can you pinpoint where?

Emotional Tools

These two sets of questions are hugely important when looking into self-evaluation, and there are ways to address each of them. Tools that can be helpful in emotion work are:

- Harvard Emotional Vocabulary Table: Google it; it is easily found and being able to articulate your feelings accurately when answering these questions will be super helpful.
- *New Bach Flower Body Maps* by Dietmar Kramer: This is a book which builds on Dr. Edward Bach's homeopathic flower remedies. Dr. Bach completed an extensive study on the link between the flower remedies and emotions. Kramer took this one step further to show where these flowers, thus emotions, tend to trigger pain or discomfort on the human body.

How did I figure out I had arrived? Even when discussing the possibility of sharing my story with you, the reader, I said, "But I don't feel like I'm standing on the mountaintop; rather that I am still playing in the foothills." *But*, I was reminded, even with the diagnosis I had been given, what it was I had recently accomplished. I rode seven hours on a motorcycle from Kentucky to Michigan and back. By myself, in construction/congested traffic, in mixed weather conditions, and with so much anxiety and excitement, thinking, *what am I really doing*? Being a ball of nerves would typically have triggered an episode of back spasms and ultimately a lockup before; yet, they didn't.

I did all of this to make it to a conference, where another very kind and wise lady provided me with a perspective shift. She called me *fearless*, and even though at the moment I automatically responded with, "No, my momma would just call it stupidity." I later remembered the conversation and said, "Wow, I did it." Even in fear, with knees knocking, even in the not knowing where I was going, and even in the not knowing how I could make everything work out. I pushed myself beyond limits my body should not have been able to tolerate, and you know what? I didn't lose even one day to recovery later. I did something that years ago my body would have stopped me dead in my tracks partway through. I did something that doctors told me I would *never* be able to do.

Getting what you want is not about being fearless. It is feeling the fear, being able to embrace *all* of the adversity, the people who speak against you, the pain that can occasionally stop you in your tracks, and the fear that will keep you stuck in your comfort zone. Everything you want, including pain freedom, is just on the other side of that. Can you see it? I can see that for you, and I long to celebrate that with you!

Fearless Tips:

- **Remember to breathe.** Easy, right? Not always. *But* deep diaphragmatic breathing allows you to focus on just the process of breathing correctly. Once you've grounded yourself to where you don't have to think about how to breathe deep, then you can continue doing so while evaluating the pain, the situation, the puzzle, the question, etc.
- **Tap into your feelings. Always remember to find a more descriptive way to articulate how you are feeling.** Even if you are only talking to yourself, say it out loud. Make sure you agree with the words you are using, as being fully *and* accurately descriptive. No *judgment*. Then repeat it one more time. At this point I would write it down, that way I could analyze it. Without fully acknowledging our feelings as good and/or bad, we cannot take the first true step to healing.
- **Every step counts.** Remember *every* step you take on your journey, no matter how small that little teeny tiny baby step is, or how *big* the fall on your face is, it is all moving forward. It is all progress, and it is all a part of the journey.

May love, light, and healing energy be ever-present on your journey to becoming fearless.

Amanda Yeary-Tiravanti, ND

Amanda Yeary-Tiravanti is an author, speaker, and a pain freedom coach. She shares her transformational journey from being dependent on prescription drugs and being in chronic pain from scoliosis to creating a life unrecognizable to where and who she used to be, serving others by bringing hope and empowering change for other women who are struggling with chronic pain. Through living what she teaches, she is a walking example of the possibilities for others. Amanda's mission is to bring hope to the hopeless, helping women understand that there are other options. Chemical dependency is not the only way, and emotions are the key to learning how.

Amanda's journey started in the small southeastern Kentucky town of Middlesboro. This is where the legacy of natural healing has its roots in initially learning from her great-great-grandmother some of the foundational herbal and common sense strategies to help with day-to-day complaints. She has maintained Mom Weaver's no-nonsense stance when helping people, with a tough-love approach to cutting though the stories of her clients, with a no-BS mentality to helping you grow past your self-imposed limits and the no-hope-just-cope messaging from modern medicine.

dramanda@gypsyhealth.org
(606) 209-1872
https://www.facebook.com/gypsyhealth
http://www.linkedin.com/in/gypsyhealth
https://twitter.com/GypsyHealthMin
https://www.instagram.com/gypsyhealthmin

TAP INTO YOUR TRUE POTENTIAL
BY ANNABEL KANDIAH

How do you think you ended up where you are today? Do you see yourself as a victim of your circumstances, drowning in your sorrows, or do you believe that you can tap into your potential and become the person you want to be?

My mission is to help strong and successful women find fulfillment in their lives. These women have had many accomplishments but they yearn for something more. Maybe they know exactly what it is or maybe it is undeveloped but they know they want something different.

I believe we all have defining moments in our lives but I also believe that we can change the course of our lives if we train our mind.

Some of my defining moments: the multiple leadership opportunities that I was given from a young age, moving to the US to go to a top MBA school, getting married and having a child in my forties, being a diplomat for a small country, and finally my journey as an entrepreneur.

I have been a leader since I was in elementary school. I have been given so many opportunities for personal growth because with leadership comes responsibilities and challenges. Some leadership positions were so rewarding it just encouraged me to help other leaders grow their potential. I recall a top leader telling me that I was considered a trusted advisor to other senior leaders and that was a strength I should be proud of. At that time, I did not fully embrace it but now I am beginning to understand what it means to truly use your gifts.

Other times, being a leader was hard as I had to bear the burden of telling people hard truths and sometimes being questioned by others about decisions I made. Being courageous was not always rewarded. It did not stop me because I felt strongly that it was my responsibility. However, I had to learn how to finesse it and I learnt how to do this from my mentors.

Some people have a straight trajectory in their career. Mine has been a series of changes but everything I have done has led me to become the person I am today. I was in the diplomatic corps for ten years. The insights, the skills I learnt along the way, the life lessons, the hardship, and the world experiences shaped my worldview. I know without a doubt that my experiences as a young leader in a small embassy prepared me for being a leadership advisor in the corporate world years later. I was twenty-six when I spent a time with the prime minister of India and other ambassadors because my ambassador and number two were away. Being exposed in this way was a gift.

Many people view negative circumstances as defining moments in their lives and others look at positive impactful events as defining moments. All of these moments combined shape our lives.

Some negative events scar you and can change the course of your life (good and bad). The one I remember vividly as a twenty-year-old was when I did not get offered honors in political science because I messed up one paper in my final exam. I had been third in my class prior to the final exams but the final exam was what counted most, and I got a B instead of an A. For some years after, I felt it defined how I was seen in the foreign service and it haunted me. Despite all that, I pushed against the grain and got offered positions and opportunities. However, it solidified my belief that I needed to have a top degree to achieve success. I grew up in the Singapore system and academic achievement was what was deemed important.

However, there has always been something inside of me that has believed that I can change my circumstances. I started to dream about getting an advanced degree that would allow me to be more successful in my career. I have always loved everything in leadership and I was exposed to so many leaders and businesses as a diplomat. I decided I wanted to get an MBA from a top school and pursue a career in talent management. I got accepted into the Fuqua School of Business at Duke University and immediately multiple doors opened up again. I was very strategic about what I wanted to study because I was interested in combining leadership development with business impact. I briefly looked at entrepreneurial studies but decided some of my other classmates were better suited. Little did I know what was lurking around the corner (in a good way).

I was so focused on my goal of talent management that when I looked for an internship, I ended up getting a full-time offer. I was offered a job in my first year and I was the first in my class to get an offer. My career had a fast trajectory after graduation and I thought this was exactly what I wanted. I had achieved what I thought was success. Again, it was how I was raised and the culture of the society I lived in for many years. I did not know that there was a whole other "world" that one could experience. An entrepreneurial world!

I climbed my way up the corporate ladder and I started to make good money, earning bigger and better titles and I really thought this is what I wanted. Who does not want success, right? With promotions and hard work, I was also asked to take on more and more responsibilities. Nobody taught me that I should not sacrifice time, freedom, and a more balanced life for success. I threw myself into being successful and other aspects of my life took a back seat. I thought you had to give up something to attain these senior positions.

While in the consulting and corporate world, I was made what I thought were promises for more promotions, more opportunities. However, the reality was that I faced some bad leadership, power decision-making, male chauvinism, and sexism. I guess I was naive but I never really expected all of that to happen to me. Well, it did! So, of course, at some point, I experienced burnout.

My life view had already started to change when I met my husband. Whenever we talked about having a family, my mind always went to having a stable income and strong foundation for retirement and investments for the kid. I would be thinking, *I need to look for a bigger job in corporate!* Yet, maybe my eyes were slowly being opened up to other possibilities as my husband's life experiences were quite different. He is an entrepreneur.

A significant turning point in my life was about six years ago. I was going to become a mother, something I longed for and really wanted. I worked through my pregnancy and some people were worried and felt I should slow down. I felt fine and I just kept going. I ended up giving birth the day after I went on leave. I thought I would want to go back to work and just continue to grow in my corporate career. I also expected to be welcomed back and continue to march upward. However, my status as a high potential leader had changed because suddenly the assumption was I would not be interested in an aspiring career. No real direct conversations, just assumptions made. Interestingly, my thinking had also changed though it took a few months for me to see it and admit it. I realized that I still wanted to impact others and give of myself but not in the same way anymore. I yearned for something different but could not pinpoint what it was at that time.

A lot happened in the first year and a half after my daughter was born. While reassessing my life and our future, my father passed away suddenly and my father in-law six months later. I did not grieve or process it right away as I had an infant and I had to take care of her. It definitely had an impact on me that I did not fully understand until a year later. It hit me that I needed to redesign my life.

One night as I sat disillusioned finishing up something for a big meeting for the Board of Directors of the company I was working for, I started to look at something a friend of mine had shared on a side income with network marketing. I kept coming back to it but it was something so foreign to me as I had never been exposed to network marketing. I finally started to research it and realized that the compensation plan was actually quite interesting. My interest had been piqued.

Several months passed and I started to think about dabbling in network marketing on the side as a source of income to see where it would take me. However, life happens when you are trying to plan for it. My department was restructured and I was given a great package to leave (having been at the company for a number of years). Wow! Was I shocked? Yes, somewhat. Was I unhappy? Not really. People find it hard to believe but the wheels had already started turning before this happened so this was not a disaster.

I have always believed that when one door shuts another opens. Since I could afford to take some time off, I decided to jump into the deep end and become an entrepreneur. Oh my! I did not know what I was getting myself into. Luckily, my husband had been an entrepreneur for nearly fifteen years and was supportive in ways he probably does not even realize, especially on days when I would think, *what did I get myself into* and I just would throw up my hands. Oh, the highs and lows and the fluctuating emotions and the learning, unlearning, and relearning that I had to do as I embraced the unknown.

The initial journey has been exciting, scary, and unexpected. However, those who know me well understand that once I decide to do something, I really jump in. I studied successful entrepreneurs and went to select masterminds retreats to figure out how this works. I sought out mentors in this new industry. One day, boom—I figured it out!

Today, my life has been transformed. My thinking has been totally changed through the mentoring and coaching I have received from my new mentors. I have reframed concepts and learnings. It is hard work to make changes to what I perceived was my path but consistency, courage, and determination has brought me to new places that I would never have imagined.

I think in many ways, I struggled in the Singapore system because I tend to go against the grain of what others wanted. I didn't just want to follow the rules in order to succeed. Something did not sit well and it took me years to realize what it was and unlearn and relearn things. Leadership development at corporate was a start but there is so much depth that I can offer the entrepreneurial world. I have coached a lot of leaders but I have taken things to a new level in the last two years and part of that is my own growth as a leader.

I am the CEO of my business and I get to write the story of my life! I lead a global growing team. Today, I stand in my own power and share with others how to tap into changing their mindset and fulfilling their potential.

Come create and architect your life with me. There is something truly wonderful waiting for you on the other side. Maybe you have dreams or maybe you forgot how to dream because you are going through your life year after year, discouraged and unfulfilled. Reach out and together we will transform your life.

This is your moment!

Tap Into Your Potential Tips:

1. Are you living your best life?
2. Do you have a dream or a vision of what you want your life to look like?
3. How do *you* define success (not others, but you)?
4. Is what you are doing fulfilling and leading to your goals?
5. Take concrete steps today toward *your* definition of success.
6. Get the right support and mentoring on your journey.
7. Take steps each day toward your success and your potential.
8. Keep going. Don't give up. Be consistent and determined.

Annabel Kandiah

Annabel Kandiah is an author and speaker as well as a leadership coach and mentor to entrepreneurs who want to step out of the corporate rat race and find fulfillment in their lives. Annabel has served in many leadership positions over the years and has a real passion to develop high-performing leaders.

Her mission is to help budding entrepreneurs become the best versions of themselves and lead the life they want. She believes that people can learn to tap into their true potential and achieve their goals and dreams. She loves this quote: "Whatever you can do, or dream you can, begin it. Boldness has genius, power and magic in it."

Annabel followed the corporate path for many years following her MBA from a top school. She saw great progression in her career but the long hours and the stress made her question what she truly wanted in life. She realized she wanted to help more people and make an impact on lives in a very different way. Success was not as important as being fulfilled. She stepped boldly into the entrepreneurial world and is now building a worldwide business.

Annabel lives in the Bay Area with her husband and her daughter. She has a passion for travel and loves meeting people from all over the world and learning about different cultures.

Social Media Links
Email Address: sannabel@outlook.com
Phone Number: 202-725-3773
Website: https://annabelkandiah.com
Facebook page(s):
https://www.facebook.com/Annabel-Tarkington-538316553289472/
Instagram: https://www.instagram.com/annabel.kandiah/

TRANSFORMATION BY FIRE
BY ARIEL BICKEL

The woman who wrote the first draft of this chapter is dead. Burned up in the fire of her Soul's transformation. More accurately, the identity of who she believed herself to be, is dead.

This is draft number four and I've already died to myself several times during the writing process. I'll die again before I'm finished, and by the time you read this, the ME who is speaking to you will be but a memory.

This isn't the chapter I envisioned myself writing when I first accepted the invitation to contribute to this book.

My current Identity - WHO I THINK I AM - is the amalgamation of all my lived experiences and learned beliefs. My soul-consciousness - WHO I BE - is inherent, timeless, and ever-evolving.

By inviting you to read this passage from my transformational saga, I hope to spark a desire in you to look inward and more deeply explore your own. I believe we elevate the world most powerfully by shifting our own consciousness first, then inviting others to join us.

At the end of this chapter, you'll find some of the most powerful principles and provocative questions which guide me in my own work. These insights are in no way exhaustive, since self-awareness, like possibilities, is INFINITE. May they serve you and your transformational journey, and you rejoice knowing that there are others here to love, guide, and support you along your way!

And so it begins...

As I sit in bed, the blank screen of my MacBook coldly staring back at me, I curse myself for once again making things so damn hard on myself. With the deadline looming over me, I feel torn between my desire to meet it, and my gut instinct to delete an entire day's worth of writing and start over. My Ego is screaming that to do so would be absolute stupidity. "*You don't have time to waste on going deeper, you're staring down the short end of a deadline, idiot!*"

Yet I can't deny the powerful Truth that's thudding in my heart. While what I've written is dramatic and impactful, it's a narrative I've been regurgitating for years: Abducted and raised under a false identity as a child, abused by my parents and ignored by adults who could have saved me, I did what was necessary to survive. The day I graduated high school, I reclaimed my birth identity and left home, determined to make it on my own and escape suffering forever. "*What a yawn! Even I'm sick of this Old Story.*"

It's dawning on me that if I only tell this part of my story, I'm effectively keeping myself trapped in my Old Identity, the helpless victim of someone else's actions. I shudder to think that this is how people will remember me. I've evolved far beyond who that girl WAS then, and I'm long overdue in updating my narrative and speaking from the Truth of WHO I AM today. **Delete.**

I begin again, and this time I'm committed to exploring the question which has sent me into a tailspin in the past: "*If I no longer define myself as an adult survivor of parental abduction and abuse, then* WHO AM I?" It's now 1:00am and I've already missed the final submission deadline. "*I sense a meltdown coming on, better not risk it or I'll never finish. I'll sleep a couple hours, keep writing, and throw myself on the mercy of the editors for an extension.*" Self-judgement dies hard. "*Keep grinding away, Ariel, give them more than they're expecting so they don't regret including you, or kick you off the project."* My Ego is oblivious to the unfair assumptions I'm heaping upon the editors.

"*Ugh! I have wisdom to share. Why can't I get out of my own way and allow it to shine through? I've focused for so long on what has been done to me, rather than how I've reclaimed my freedom and power, that I'm still talking about myself like I'm a victim.*"

Fast forward a few hours...I'm reading over what I last wrote...And I'm realizing that I'm not THAT woman anymore, either. "*What the hell is happening to me?*" **Delete.**

It's one thing to listen to spiritual teachers expound on the virtues of personal transformation, and quite another thing to find your own Ego laying on the spiritual operating table. **Transformation, it turns out, is a messy process.**

"*Shit. WHO is showing up to write this chapter? How can I inspire others with my story of breaking free to stand in my power when so much of what I've believed to be reality up until now keeps shifting AS I'm writing?*" Nausea is flooding my stomach. This feels insane, like hopping onto an untamed mustang and hanging on for dear life while it runs wild, hurtling forward at full throttle. I'm feeling simultaneously freaked out and incredibly free. I have no idea where this creature is taking me, I just know I'd better hang on.

I need a walk, to clear my head. I fear the worst: "*Once again I'm going to ruin my chances at earning the love and acceptance of others because I can't get my shit together!*" Ego has me comparing myself to my peers, in an attempt to shame me into hopping off this unpredictable ride and playing small. "*You had a shot and you screwed it up. They're going to reject you. See, you're not ready for the big time. Stay here with me, I'll keep you safe.*"

Then suddenly I feel like laughing. Safety, at this point, is an illusion. This untamed beast is heading for the big cliff ahead and the only control I have is to choose how I experience the drop. "*Perhaps THIS would be a good time to practice surrendering to WHAT IS. Ha!*"

I feel a shift happening inside me as the beast and I hurtle off the edge. Something heavy is falling away. I release a deep sigh of relief.

Back in front of the screen. Experiencing the sweet release from my attachment to the outcome of this chapter, I know what I get to do next...

My friend answers my call right away and now I'm sobbing into the phone as I allow my anger, guilt, shame, and self-judgement to flow. I'm releasing a sea of old pain and she's quietly holding space while I grieve. My body's reassuring me that there's nothing left to do but surrender to WHAT IS, to let go of needing approval and being included in the book.

I decide to get curious: "*What if I simply let go of my belief that mistakes and failures are real things? What is available for me if I choose to shift my perspective to come from a place of gratitude for this experience?*"

With each deep breath I take now, I'm experiencing a lightening of my spirit. "*There's no one I need to BE, nothing I need to prove.*"

Now I exist beyond time, space, and physical form. I visualize myself encased in a hard shell of darkness, which is shattering into a million shards and falling away. I'm not merely visualizing this, I'm FEELING it. My Old Identity is disintegrating around me. My only job in this moment - this timeless NOW - is to stay present and hold myself with compassion and love.

"*Trust yourself. You're experiencing an awakening at a level previously unknown to you.*"

It's profound to experience the death of my Old Self, as she clings for dear life to people, places, experiences, and beliefs. How can I possibly say good-bye to her after all she's brought me through?

"*Remain still. It's not your job to go after your Old Identity and kill her off. It's your job to love her, wrap her in compassion, and bless her, as she gently surrenders and integrates as a part of your Whole Self.*"

I'm experiencing so many Breakdowns/Breakthroughs, I barely have time to process one before the next one is hitting me. The more I sit still and deeply listen to what's arising, the more powerful the insights that are coming through. This feels exhilarating and frustrating all at the same time because it's a challenge to write quickly enough to keep up with all that I'm experiencing. I so desperately want to share this all with you, to allow you to live this experience through me!

I KNOW that this is the story I'm meant to be sharing. I want you to really feel that it's healthy to fall apart and get messy. When you dig out from the rubble of toppled identities and broken expectations, you'll emerge an even greater version of yourself than you ever dreamed possible.

The words which are flowing through my consciousness to the screen are taking on new meaning and energy, I'm constantly being shown new ways of perceiving things.

As I'm translating my radical insights, intimate truths, and fiery wisdom onto the screen, I'm in awe of how far I've come. There have been so many times, over the years, that the changes appeared so small - almost imperceptible - that I wanted to give up, check out, even die. "*Why do therapy, trainings, and self-help tools seem to work for others but not for me? Am I beyond help, too damaged, unlovable, and flawed to have the adventurous, successful, fulfilling life I yearn for?*"

I hadn't learned yet to TRUST that there are powerful forces at work that we don't always see, and that none of our efforts are wasted. When we least expect it, we find ourselves integrating and elevating at lightning speed. The learning, growing, and evolving is never finished. Life is about so much more than survival. In this very moment, I'm expanding far beyond anything I could have ever imagined possible.

I'm trusting my Identity as a Woman Of Fire, Warrior Goddess, and Fire Siren, even as I'm learning that WHO I AM is an ever-evolving consciousness burning within and flooding throughout this organic form.

SO ARE YOU. You're precious, perfectly imperfect, and ever-changing. You already carry all your answers within you. Please take this in and allow it to settle deep in your heart.

15 Incendiary Love Notes To Fuel Your Transformation

1. Stop Looking Outwards For The Answers You Think You Need.
2. Stop Waiting For Someone Else To Rescue Or Validate You.
3. Allow Yourself To Be Pulled By What You Love, Not Pushed By What You Fear.
4. Celebrate Everything.
5. Practice Radical Gratitude.
6. You Are Only This Moment.
7. Schedule Playtime First.
8. Prioritize Spending Time Alone, Getting Still, And Connecting With Your Inner Self.
9. The First Person Who Gets To Love You And BE A Stand For You Is You.
10. You Are Your Own Source Of Love And Abundance.
11. Practice Fierce Compassion And Messy Vulnerability.
12. Allow Your Old Identity To Die To Itself Constantly.
13. Trust That Your Life Is Unfolding Perfectly, Right On Time.
14. You Are A Whole Human, Stop Splintering Your Personal and Professional Identities.
15. Let Go Of Criticism - Others Who Don't Get Your Big Vision Are Likely Intimidated Or Threatened By Your Authenticity.

7 Provocative Questions To Ignite Your Inner Fire

1. What does living in alignment with your Purpose, Highest Self, and Big Vision, feel like for you?
2. How would your life be different if you gave yourself permission to live fully, according to your Truth?
3. Who are you still asking for permission to BE your Authentic Self, and why?
4. How could embracing your integrated Whole Self supercharge your life?
5. What are you closing yourself off from receiving, and why?
6. What's something exciting you're feeling called to do, but are allowing excuses to get in the way of?
7. What would life be like if you chose to let everything be Easy?

Ariel Bickel

Ariel Bickel is the Visionary Rebel and Founding Instigator of The Shifters Collective and WOFILAs (Women Of Fire In a Life Aflame) movements. Her paradigm-shifting approach, and The signature program, Becoming the Fire, is a dynamic and liberating way to support profound personal transformation and shift in those ready to dive deep into their own awakening. Abducted by her father and living under a false identity until she was 18, Ariel knows it is critical for you to discover and integrate your Whole Human, and to embrace your own inner knowing. Ariel approaches each day as a unique opportunity to awaken to self-love, cultivate collective joy, and practice deep reconnection with our natural world. For three decades, she has dedicated her life to advancing the ideals of justice, joy, peace, abundance, and fulfillment for all through her activism and political work. She has reached thousands through her coaching, public speaking, writing, training, advocacy, and organizing. Her daily focus is on practicing, teaching, and leading herself and others through personal transformation, to know the inner truth that makes each of us free. Her message of reclaiming and redefining your own identity, power, and path, in this critical moment of time, shows us opportunities to elevate and grow our collective, conscious wellbeing. She is a powerful coach for coaches and thought leaders, artists and creatives, social entrepreneurs and activists, healers and transformational visionaries; she inspires and transforms with her fire, wisdom, and persistence. Ariel's unwavering commitment to living and practicing an unapologetic, free, and fierce life is her lifeblood; her fidelity to raw, real, authentic awakening, expression, and contribution is the bedrock of her life's calling. She is committed to helping others to live, lead, and thrive from a place of fierce compassion and radical gratitude.

SOCIAL MEDIA & CONTACT INFO
Email Address: ariel@arielbickel.com
Phone Number: 505-321-6867
Website: arielbickel.com
Facebook page(s): https://www.facebook.com/BEingArielBickel/
LinkedIn Page: https://www.linkedin.com/in/ariel-bickel-935aa07/
Twitter handle: @atbickel
Instagram: https://www.instagram.com/atbickel/

GIVE ME SOME SUNSHINE
BY ASHIMA GIRI

I was thirteen years old when I was presented a huge opportunity to move back to America. My grandmother had lung cancer, stage three, and my family and I decided to move to take care of her and further my education in the states. I was born in Fremont but I grew up in India. Taking care of my dying grandmother at a young age and watching her die contributed a lot to my depression. While taking care of her, I had to go to school and the change of environment was so drastic that it was very hard for me to adjust to it. And as I went through life, my depression got worse which really led to me being suicidal.

It was sophomore year in high school when I almost ended my life. I felt absolutely horrible. That feeling, I would never wish upon anyone. **I felt so empty. I felt like nothing mattered; it genuinely felt like my life was going nowhere and like my life didn't matter. Although part of me wanted to die, I knew I truly wanted to be saved.** So I went to my school counselor and she took the right actions in order to save me. She called my parents and my parents were in complete shock and disbelief. No parent wants to receive a phone call saying their child wants to commit suicide. I'm so glad she called them and sat them down because if she hadn't, I wouldn't be able to see the next day. Thank god for my parents taking it seriously and taking the right steps in order to heal me mentally and emotionally.

When it comes to Indian families, mental health is not talked about or acknowledged and it's considered weak to have any sort of mental illness. I'm so grateful that my parents had taken me seriously and had taken the right actions and didn't say, "Why do you feel like that? It could be so much worse; you have nothing to be upset about." **Although I'm very privileged, life still hands you hard times to grow and some people don't even make it out alive. I almost didn't. What helped me was the support from my family, therapy, and changing my diet to a much healthier one.** I never realized how much diet can change your mood and hormones in a good way. It was a hard journey because when junior year came around, I hit that point again. It wasn't because of school but it definitely contributed to it.

Whether we like to believe it or not, high school is one of the worst things to go through; everyone says how fun those four years are and how you'll regret not doing anything and being involved in high school. But, from my experience, it's the complete opposite—those four years don't make or break your life, those years are meant to realize who you are and not what you want to do for the rest of your life. That adds a lot of pressure on teens; just four years to make a life-changing decision when teenagers are already going through enough changes? It can be too much. Choosing to go to the community college really helped take off the pressure of going to a four-year college right away. I realized I needed to take care of my mental health and choosing to go to CC really helped me. **Without the help of my parents and close friends, I wouldn't have been able to get through the worst moments of my life.** I share this so any of you with a history of depression or struggle know that you are not alone and I'll share tips I discovered that help me stay balanced, peaceful, and positive.

There are more life events that contributed to my depression, like my accident. It was the most terrifying and traumatic accident I've ever been in. My car was flipped 180 degrees on the left side and I thought the car was on fire. I survived with minimal injuries but the fear of that experience had a lasting effect on me. I was shaken up for a long time and I couldn't drive for a while. All I could do was lay in bed for weeks. I wasn't able to do much other than binge-watch Netflix and cry. And as you can imagine, my depression got worse because I had nothing to do and the accident would replay in my head over and over again. I would have nightmares about it if I didn't watch TV while I fell asleep at night. In my dreams I would feel stuck and like I couldn't move, just like how I felt when I was in the flipped car. The scene kept replaying in my head like a broken record; it almost made me feel like I should've died in that car accident but people kept reminding me that there was a reason I didn't. That's true; I don't know what my purpose in life is yet, but I will find it soon. When I was going through it, I saw no point in living but people around me kept me going. Although I cried myself to sleep every night, some nights, it felt like I was watching myself crying in bed and I couldn't do anything about it.

The hardest part of going through rough times is that you have to feel it in order to get over it and going through it is so hard because it feels like it will never end. But, it does. Life may not get back on track right away, but we need to be alive to see things work out. Sometimes, the future's a little blurry and it's not fun. My biggest problem is uncertainty: you never know when people walk out of your life, you never know who you might meet, and you never know who might just stay there forever. With that, you can't do anything but accept it. **Life's hard but the universe will never put you in a situation you can't handle. I think that's the hardest thing to accept—yeah, the universe or God will never put you in a situation you can't handle, but when you're going through it, it's hard to see that.**

Today, I'm happy to share that I have a powerful community of support. When we are going through a hard time we tend to neglect ourselves and our feelings because it's hard to pay attention to your heart when everything around you is falling apart. This is why writing can help; you don't have to be someone else or something else on paper that only you are going to see. It's just you; being honest with yourself can be hard but also rewarding. I've learned that everyone is you pushed out so if you don't take care of yourself then that just tells the universe and the world that it's okay for people to step on you and treat you like crap. If you don't love yourself, others won't either. Society has taught us to take care of others first and put yourself last, when it should be the other way around. **It's okay to say no to things you don't want to do; it's okay to stay in and take care of yourself; it's okay to love yourself. That's when we can be strongest.**

If you're dealing with someone who is depressed or suicidal or any other mental illness, don't leave them in the dark and don't push them away. If you don't know how to support, just sit there and listen. That's the best thing you can do. **The hard times in my life really showed me my strengths when I felt the weakest.** I didn't see my strengths until I was crying on the floor, thinking I'd be better if I were dead. Do I feel like that sometimes still? Yes, but I can handle it better. I still surprise myself knowing how much I can handle.

Mental health awareness is important; if we don't talk about it then we're going to continue to see the suicide rates go up, hear about someone dying by killing themselves on the news, or keep losing people. We need to change; it doesn't matter where you come from, what family you belong to, or how society perceives mental health. But, mental health is just as important as physical health. If only everyone treated mental health just as seriously, we wouldn't have so many deaths due to suicide. If we make talking about our struggles normal then it wouldn't be weird if your child/friend/someone comes home saying they are depressed.

Things that have helped me are: going to therapy, spending time with loved ones, taking time for myself, facing my feelings by journaling, trying to do things that I previously loved like dance, writing, working out, drawing, etc. While it is extremely hard to do things that you love when you're feeling low, you have to fight back sometimes to feel just a little bit better. While medications are an option for severe depression, I couldn't go down that path. I wanted to get better naturally and changing my diet, talking, and exercising really helped me. Working out helps to get the endorphins going; it's a healthy way to cope with things. You gain more confidence because your body starts looking like you want it to. It doesn't have to be mundane—it can be fun like dancing, biking, boxing, hiking, etc.

Here are my tips to helping you find sunshine when you are feeling down:

1. Let people know so you can get help and support if needed.
2. Let people and support into your life. Build a community of support.
3. Journal and gain clarity about feelings so that they can be processed and released.
4. Choose your friends carefully.

5. Watch the foods you eat. Some can help you feel more balanced and positive whereas others can have the opposite effect.
6. Move: exercise, walk, dance, and have fun moving your body.
7. Discover what matters most to you.
8. Discover and appreciate your strengths.
9. Take regular mental health checkups, just like we have physical checkups.

Ashima Giri

Ashima Giri is a nineteen-year-old college student and the owner of a clothing line advocating mental health awareness and suicide prevention called Don't Die Clothing. Twenty percent of the profits go to suicide prevention organizations like San Francisco Suicide Prevention, The Trevor Project, and National Suicide Prevention Lifeline. The purpose of the brand is to let people struggling with any mental illness know that they are not alone and that there's hope. She was only seventeen years old when this clothing brand was born and has impacted teenagers across the country. You can visit the website at www.dontdieclothing.com

Social Media:
Instagram: _dontdieclothing
Website: dontdieplease.bigcartel.com
Email: dontdieclothing18@gmail.com or ashigiri00@gmail.com

BREAKING FREE FROM MENTAL ILLNESS
BY ERNESTO MEDINA

My personal story and struggle began at the age of seventeen and falls into the medical category of mental illness and psychiatry. More specifically my struggle was with what roughly 17 million other Americans also suffer from: clinical depression. The difference: my depression came along with Generalized Anxiety Disorder and Panic Disorder all at the same time. So, not only was I dealing with all the symptoms of depression, I was constantly anxious about everything and was having multiple panic attacks a day for no apparent reason or trigger.

Now, anyone who has experienced chronic anxiety with panic attacks knows how difficult and debilitating it can be just to try and function in your day-to-day life. Add on top of that, the stress and pressures of life, work, kids, a demanding boss—or in my case, demanding parents who expected nothing less than excellence. In my case, at seventeen years old, my only contributing life stressors were trying to keep my first-ever high school girlfriend happy, trying to keep my strict and controlling parents from grounding me every week for wanting to be out of the house all day, showing up to my part-time job at a dental office, and finishing my community college transfer requirements to transfer to a four-year university as fast as possible and get out of my parents' house. Looking back now as a thirty-two-year-old adult, my life stressors seem insignificant, but to a young adult living in that moment, trying to decide what to do with the rest of their life, career and yearning for complete freedom from parental control is everything.

Needless to say, my ability to function and live my life became very difficult. I was having panic attacks so frequently that I could not even go to a friend's house, go to my part-time job, or attend classes at my community college without having a full-blown attack multiple times a day. It became so extreme, at that time, I was taking a summer calculus class that I completely failed because I would get so much anxiety before a test that I could not sit in class long enough to finish the exam. That was a big low point for me and likely the peak of my declining health, depression, anxiety, and possibly failing my future life plans to transfer to a university and start a career in healthcare helping other people. By the way, if you have never experienced a full-blown panic attack or know what one feels like, imagine your worst fear, like being trapped in a box and buried alive. That fear and panic response you start to feel, multiply that by ten and imagine that feeling randomly hit you multiple times per day without warning and without provocation. This gives you a sense of what it is like living with chronic anxiety and panic attacks.

I think that's enough with the negativity and sadness, don't you? What I really enjoy sharing is how I came to better understand my health, how my journey of conquering mental illness played out, how my experiences may help others like me, and how my experiences ended up making me the healthcare provider I am today.

My healing and recovery did not come in the form of some spiritual awakening. It also did not come from prayers, religion, spiritual retreats, etc. I don't mean to downplay those things as they are very useful therapies that work for some people. I often recommend patients to explore the use of meditation and prayer if they are so inclined to help with their healing in cases of autoimmune diseases, physical and psychological trauma, and even degenerative brain diseases like Alzheimer's. But my journey was quite different. At seventeen years old, I felt as though I should have been at the peak of my health and fitness. I was a high school athlete playing soccer, wrestling, and running cross country. After graduation I continued weight training three or four times per week and eating what I thought was a healthy diet. I did not and had not used drugs or alcohol at all, yet I was struggling with debilitating health issues. I was frustrated with myself, my brain, and my body for getting sick, but more than anything, I was determined, very determined, to get better. I know now, after working with multiple patients over the years, that if one lacks a strong will and determination to get better, oftentimes they won't get better despite receiving the best treatments medicine can offer. It is like the saying goes, "You can lead a horse to water, but you can't force it to drink" (unknown).

I first discovered I was suffering from depression after taking an online self-assessment test I found after a quick web search. I knew something was wrong and had been wrong with me for weeks. I had no motivation to do anything. I felt constant guilt for no reason and sleeping felt like the only relief from my depressive mood. Shortly after the anxiety and panic attacks set in as well. Every time I had an argument with my girlfriend my depression would worsen and I preferred to isolate myself over trying to reason with her and work it out. Likewise, every time my parents grounded me or took away my car privileges instead of arguing or trying to prove my point and justify what I did, I would just give up without a fight. I literally had no will to fight for myself in any sense. But, it wasn't all bad with my parents. Despite being strict, demanding, and overbearing on me, they were very good listeners. When I brought up the self-assessment test and showed them the results they immediately helped me find professional help. I started seeing a cognitive behavioral therapist or what I like to call, "talk therapy." Basically, you go and talk about your feelings to a professional. I found it incredibly ridiculous at first. I wasn't accustomed to talking about my feelings to anyone and we spent the first few sessions literally just staring at each other. Every time I said something his response was, "How does that make you feel?" After a few sessions I realized you only get out of this type of therapy what you put into it. I started taking notes of how I was feeling every day, noting potential triggers to my anxiety and depression as well as strange habits I had developed since becoming depressed. Once I started heading into the sessions prepared with notes about topics to discuss, we started to discover many things. As it turned out, I had a lot of built-up anger over the past year as a senior in high school. Having my first-ever high school girlfriend and friends that were driving everywhere, I wanted to be out of the house and social all the time. I wanted to have a reasonable curfew that didn't require me to be home by 10 p.m. on weekends, but my parents were not having it at all. They became more and more strict, demanding and controlling. If I acted out, argued or talked back, I would be punished. The more I argued, the more severe the punishments would be. No car, no going out, no seeing the girlfriend, no parties, etc. As it turns out, my therapist helped me discover that built-up anger that is constantly internalized and not expressed in a healthy way becomes depression. It is common for depression and anxiety to come in a pair—how lucky I was to get both.

Despite having these newfound discoveries about myself, I was still struggling with the constant anxiety and panic attacks. The therapist recommended I talk to a psychiatrist about it. This of course led to a prescription of antidepressant medication and an anxiety medication know as Xanax, a benzodiazepine medication that is being discovered to have high potential for addiction and dependency. The medications did help temporarily control my anxiety. I was pretty much a zombie when I took them and would take two- to three-hour naps afterward from the extreme drowsiness they would cause. The medications helped me function in short increments of time, but were by no means a permanent fix. I was determined to find a better solution.

In the sessions with my therapist, I also learned that I could gain some kind of control of my depressive mood and anxiety through more intense exercise. High intensity strength training six to seven days a week became my natural medication. I could strategically time my workouts before anxiety-provoking activities like school, exams, or an outing with friends and not be so anxious. If something triggered my anxiety to drastically increase, I would head to the gym the first chance I could get to bring the anxiety back down. When I felt good, I would still exercise to prevent my anxiety from getting out of control in the future. It became a very useful tool for me and greatly helped my depressive mood as well. I had to make exercise part of my daily life if I wanted to function to the best of my ability.

I also discovered the power of consistent, restful sleep which I now know is called sleep hygiene. Recent research in neurology and immunology has shown that getting eight to ten hours of good quality sleep allows your immune system to clear metabolic waste in the brain. In a way, it allows your brain to reset for the coming day. I didn't know this at the time, but I did notice if I slept less or had poor quality sleep I would wake up the next morning very anxious. I would not even get out of bed and my anxiety levels were already higher than usual. Sleep hygiene is another concept I teach patients who are dealing with neurological issues or immune issues such as autoimmune diseases.

The last two things I discovered that are big contributing factors to mental health are stress and good nutrition. Stress I discovered early on because arguments, confrontations, and stressful school work with deadlines would all trigger worsening of my depressive mood and spike my anxiety immediately. Stress is an inevitable part of our life, so I will expand a bit more later on how I worked at improving my tolerance to life stressors to go on to finish graduate school and open my own integrative health center. The nutritional aspect of mental health is something I did not understand until after I graduated from chiropractic school and got involved in a post-graduate program studying clinical neuroscience and functional neurology. The concept of nutrition for mental health is still decades away from becoming mainstream medicine, but it has recently been coined "nutritional psychiatry." The concept of nutrition for mental health has been around for decades, especially in the functional medicine and integrative health world, but to have a small group of integrative psychiatrists finally catch up to the research and call it nutritional psychiatry is exciting and promising for the future.

In the end, after several years of keeping balance in what I call the mental health pentagon of stress, nutrition, sleep, supplements, and exercise, I was able to conquer my mental health struggles and get off all medications. Unfortunately, I didn't get much help from any of my medical doctors in doing this. Any time I brought up lowering the dosage of my medications to eventually stop them altogether they brushed me off. They were not supportive of this in the least. I have come to find out that most patients prescribed antidepressant and anxiety medications never end up stopping them. It ends up being a lifelong prescription. The idea of having an exit strategy to come off those medications is never discussed or even hinted at. The thought is never placed in a patient's mind so they never strive to work toward that goal. Needless to say, I had to figure out on my own how to taper off the dosages without side effects or withdrawal symptoms. The antidepressant medication was the hardest to completely stop due to withdrawal side effects I kept experiencing. It was a chiropractic neurologist trained in functional medicine that I met while a chiropractic student who eventually helped stop the withdrawal side effects from the medication using a targeted supplement program. The experiences I had with that doctor was one of the driving factors that motivated me to study clinical neuroscience and functional medicine and apply it in my own health center.

Here are my tips to support you on your journey to break free:

1. Never lose the desire to keep getting better
2. Express your feelings in a healthy way
3. Keep constant balance in the mental health pentagon forever
4. Develop an exit and improvement strategy from where you are currently to where you want to be
5. Find mentors or doctors that are willing to listen and guide you
6. You can break free! Just keep taking steps in the right direction.

Dr. Ernesto Medina

Dr. Ernesto Medina is the founder of the Bay Area Health and Wellness Center in San Jose, California, a functional medicine and neurology-based health center focused on helping people with chronic unresolved health struggles that conventional medicine has been unable to help. After receiving his bachelor's degree from the University of California, San Diego in 2009, Dr. Medina immediately went on to pursue a career in health care. In 2012 he graduated from Life Chiropractic College West in Hayward, California and went straight into clinical practice.

He is currently a member of the International Association of Functional Neurology and Rehabilitation and the Kharrazian Institute where he continues to stay up to date with the latest research and clinical applications in functional medicine and clinical neuroscience to better serve his patients.

Social Media Links:
Email: info@bayareahealthandwellness.com
408-755-5710
Website: https://bayareahealthandwellness.com/
Facebook: https://www.facebook.com/bayareahealthandwellness
LinkedIn:
https://www.linkedin.com/in/ernesto-medina-dc-1875227a/
YouTube channel: Bay Area Health & Wellness Center
Instagram: @dr.ernesto_medina_dc

SECTION 2:

Embrace the Journey

FROM PAIN TO PROFOUND PURPOSE
BY INDU AGGARWAL

"The wound is the place where light enters you."
Rumi

I always felt that there was a specific purpose to life but had no idea how to go about finding mine. Consciously I kept an open mind, felt that I was responsible for my own health and had keen interest in holistic medicine. **Then one day, it all started with a back pain that hit me like a lightning bolt that could have destroyed me if I was not grounded!**

I remember that it was in August 2005 and I was looking forward to our trip to Eastern Europe. One day, just after my gym visit, a little tension started in my back. By that night, it had turned into a full-blown, stabbing pain. I did the usual things: resting, icing, and topical ointments but this pain was not relenting. It felt like broken glass inside my back with pieces going down to my hip. Since the trip was around the corner, I decided to get a quick diagnosis. I was certain that I had either broken a bone or had a tear somewhere. To my disappointment, x-rays did not show anything broken and doctors told me that I was having sciatica pain. I had never heard or experienced such sharp pain except during labor. In fact, this pain felt like childbirth every day but nothing was getting delivered! I did go on vacation while icing and suffering for two weeks. Sitting was a torture; standing was the next worst thing. Lying down and walking felt better but pain was constantly present. I literally needed to sit on top of ice and use local numbing ointments to get any relief.

The sciatic nerve is the largest nerve in the body that starts from the lower spine, passes under the hip, and ends at the heel of the foot. You are expected to feel pain whenever the nerve is pinched, whether at its origin or anywhere along its path. Most people feel it in the lower back, under the hip, but it can radiate all the way through the leg and heel.

Back in town and back to work, the torture continued. Stronger pain killers, physical therapy, and even the cortisone shot would not alleviate the pain. Basically, I was doing the "normal" thing of resisting the pain, masking it and feeling helpless. **When back surgery was proposed as the best solution, it was a rude awakening and my desperation increased to find an alternative solution. My perspective moved from the problem to the solution. And a journey inward started.**

Breakthrough #1: While educating myself more on the sciatica pain, I discovered that it can be triggered when there are sudden emotional or financial changes in life. Now I really got curious and started the detective work to find the cause. At a conscious level, there "seemed" to be no big changes in my life or "nothing" that I could not handle. But a loop of self-reflection opened up. I even heard a small voice in my head: "You can fix it." **This perspective changed my focus from "why" to "what" and changed my life. I was no longer scared of the pain and felt that there was a story to uncover.** I was simply making observations and some of them were very interesting. I could literally feel my pain level go up and down with my mental state and the emotional states of people around me. If I was talking to somebody I didn't like, the pain would escalate and I could literally feel who was a "pain in the butt." I started enjoying the humor in the midst of this pain.

Breakthrough #2: It was December and my patience was running out after four months of pain. I was losing hope and then, the second breakthrough came. I went to the gym to put my membership on hold and met a trainer from Australia. He was a physical therapist by profession but could not practice since he did not have US certification yet. He told me that western doctors will not be able to fix this problem. He knew of a technique called "myofascial release." He did the "unofficial release" for me and it brought some relief to my pain. **Now I was convinced that the pain is like a string stuck under a heavy rock and it can be released. Question is, how?**

Breakthrough #3: I was still quite upset because I felt that New Year was around the corner and I can't party or dance due to my back. **One day, I decided to put music on, let go of my fear and dance even if it breaks my back or leg. I danced alone for an hour and when I stopped, the pain had miraculously disappeared. This was the "eureka" moment of my life!** I did not believe it; I was sure that it will be reappearing in the morning. But it did not come and I enjoyed New Year's Eve dancing. I was pain-free for two months and then, suddenly, pain returned at the end of January without any warning and this time, dancing would not fix it!

Breakthrough #4: Since I had seen the pain come and go mysteriously, I was quite certain that there was an emotional component to the pain. This was my best clue and one day, I was able to unfold it like a secret written on a paper and buried deep in my subconscious. Wow, I had access to the story of my pain. It was like a door opening and light entering a dark chamber. I knew that I was angry over a sudden change in our life due to a relationship but I thought that it was just the matter of coping with it. The situation had rendered me powerless and made me angry but I must have buried it so deep inside. **For the first time, I realized that when the stress is too high for the mind to process, it results in physical symptoms so that we experience it as pain**. It was anger, guilt, and betrayal all wrapped in a package. **When I had the courage to see it, I clearly saw the repressed anger under my first episode of pain and guilt under the second episode of pain.**

Breakthrough #5: Even when I was quite certain of emotional causes of my pain, I did not know what kind of treatment to use to clear my emotional traps and energy blockages. How do I lift the stones and release my pinched nerve? Then another inner clue came as a suggestion that I needed to get away from home to clear my energy block. Sometimes, the prescription to travel has a very valid reason; it makes you think things differently and you are in a different energetic field. When an opportunity came to travel to Japan and China, I decided to go in spite of my pain. Imagine sitting in a ten-hour plane ride on top of an ice bag, drugged and almost sleepwalking. I am glad that I had the courage to tolerate it all. **One thing was certain: whenever I talked about my pain, my focus was on the solution. "I know that I can fix it."** A fellow traveler reassured me that she can see the power in my aura to fix this problem! She became my lifelong friend.

Breakthrough #6: During the customer visit in China, I casually mentioned the reason for my continuous walking in the meeting. **A fellow engineer asked me to read a book called *Mind over Back Pain* if I wanted to be pain-free for the rest of my life! Another clue that the mind has a lot to do with our pains.** The night before our departure, I got a massage from a Chinese lady. She did not speak English and I did not know Chinese. We talked using pictures and I am not sure what her technique was. It felt like something similar to mayo-fascial release. It felt good but the pain was still there. **After another ten-hour flight, I got off the plane and finally, I had left the pain behind and this time for good. A miracle indeed, I was out of pain after nine months!** I did read the recommended book and the best thing I learnt is that medical diagnosis will show spinal problems for lot of people, but very few of them show up as physical symptoms. So a diagnosis can reveal a weakness but does not manifest into pain without a trigger.

Breakthrough #7: It was clear to me that there was still a bigger purpose of this pain. I still needed to find a lifelong and systematic method to uncover causes of our health issues and also be of help to other people. After showing so much courage, suffering, and seeing a miracle, there was no going back. I needed to integrate this new knowledge in my life. **My search culminated in a direction when a visitor (a friend's cousin) from England told me about the BodyTalk System by Body Talk Association.** In my first treatment session, I felt that this was the energetic healing that I could and would use going forward. I started taking classes and became a Certified BodyTalk practitioner in 2012. I truly believe that my bodymind had discovered this modality intuitively even before I ever heard about it. It is a type of healthcare designed by your body to help you. I also became a corporate mindfulness teacher and thoroughly enjoy teaching this subject to teens and adults. I moved from an engineering career and launched my own business. **I love to inspire people toward their own healing path with a combination of mindfulness and BodyTalk System.**

Pain is inevitable but suffering is optional. To claim your own healing power, don't get attached to your physical diagnosis and use more than traditional solutions. Keep an open mind and be very aware that you talk of your pain and disease with the specific focus on finding a solution. In other words, stop yourself from being a victim and glorifying your condition for the sake of sympathy. ***Unconsciously, you can fall in love with your pain and it can become your identity.*** **Believe that a unique solution is possible for you and you are worth it.** You know your body and life better than anyone else, so claim your own healing power first. Then, ask the universe for help, look for clues, and let go of the fear. Miracles do happen; believe in them. Meditate regularly, get in touch with your inner world and your purpose, and try a BodyTalk session. I hope that you never have to go through such pain but if you do, please remember that these pains you feel are messengers. Listen to them. And don't forget to dance!

To Claim Your Healing Power:

1. Don't get attached to your physical diagnosis. Pay attention to your emotional state.
2. Use more than traditional solutions.
3. Become aware of self-talk. Don't be a victim and start believing that cure is not possible.
4. Focus on solutions and listen when new options are suggested. Try them.
5. Trust that a unique solution is possible for you.
6. Claim your own healing power. Surrender and let it come.
7. Actively replace fear with trust.
8. Meditate, ask for help, and listen to what your body is saying.
9. Remember to unwind, relax, and do the dance.

Indu Aggarwal

Indu Aggarwal is a mindfulness teacher, motivational speaker who is also certified in a revolutionary energetic healing method, the BodyTalk System. Indu began her journey into complementary medicine in the midst of her stressful job as an engineering manager in the Silicon Valley, twins at home and debilitating back pain.. When faced with the prospect of invasive back surgery, she turned to more holistic approach, to get to the root cause of her problem. Her severe back pain became a journey which eventually culminated in the courage to her lifelong healing, even from other chronic problems.

Indu provides unique coaching sessions using a combination of mindfulness and BodyTalk self-healing method. Indu loves to inspire and empower people on their own healing journey. She seeks to show you how you can take your own chronic pain or "disease" as a message and not only reduce or get rid of it, but identify the root cause of why you had the problem to begin with! From her personal experience, Indu believes that it is often "the deepest pain which inspires you to grow into your highest self," and looks forward to empowering you into purposeful life beyond pain.

Email: indu@bodytalksmindlistens.com
Phone: (408) 359-7909
www.bodytalksmindlistens.com
FB: Easy healing with Indu
LinkedIn: Indu Aggarwal
YouTube channel: bodytalksmindlistens

FINDING YOUR VOICE: REMEMBER, RECAST, BREATHE AND JUMP IN

BY JEANNE ALFORD

Has this happened to you? You find a quiet moment—I know, precious few exist in this distracting, fast pace world. But that quiet moment. Then in your mind's eye, a flash pops. It's a scene from your past. A memory of a significant event. These are more than prized moments, they can be prophetic too.

Every once in a while, I get a flash of a memory. A childhood drama unfolds—first in the back of my mind, then it shoots itself straight into my consciousness. My heart races a little, I gulp in a breath and I remember, that was then. To me, it seems like a mini panic attack. My breathing stops for that moment, I feel my heartbeat pounding. Then I come to my senses and remember "the story."

My mother volunteered for "hot dog day" at my brother and two sisters' school. She packed up the rest of us—me, my little brother, and my infant sister—and drove to their school. She told us it was Thursday and she needed us to behave while she served hot dogs to all the kids. My brother and I got excited because we loved hot dogs. I believe the kids were served a hot dog, on a bun, with a bag of chips and a carton of milk for the grand total of twenty-five cents.

We arrived at the school. My mother trained us well. I held onto one side of the stroller and my brother held onto the other. We knew what was expected. Then I saw her. To four-year-old me, in my limited life experience, I saw an alien robot. I immediately let go of the stroller and hid behind my mother's skirt. It was considered a "full skirt" by 1960s design standards and that meant there was a lot of fabric for me to hide behind.

What I saw was a real life Rosie the Robot. Rosie was the robot maid on the popular Jetson's cartoon series. For a four-year-old, that was real. But to see this creature up close and personal, I was terrified. That was my perception.

I was told to come over and say hi to Sister.

I wouldn't budge.

The nun, who wore a long black habit, maxi length, with a large black and white headpiece covering her hair, smiled at me and said my name.

I saw no feet. She must be rolling around like Rosie, right?

My older siblings saw the commotion and came over. They did what older siblings do. They laughed. "That's just Sister Mary," they chimed at once. My mother sternly told me to come out and be polite.

Shaking like a leaf, I reached out my hand to shake the nun's and said a very jittery hello.

Here's the rub, it's my story. However, I was four. The details, like the quarter for the hot dogs, and the name of the nun, got filled in over the years by others. So was it really my story? Was I as frightened as I recall? I remember the fear and the uneasy conclusion. I say that because, when that little gem of a memory pops up, that's what I am experiencing.

Maya Angelou said, "I've learned that people will forget what you said, people will forget what you did, but people will never forget how you made them feel." She was so right!

What brings it up—this slice of childhood? Usually, I get this flash of insight before I get up in front of a crowd. As a teen, when my church choir performed at concerts. As a young professional manager, when I needed to present to a client or a group of executives. To this day, before I get up to speak or deliver a communications workshop. I relegate it to "the jitters." More recently, I've started to meditate picturing that little girl cowering behind her mother's skirt as she stares down the alien robot. I put my arms around her and said, "Let's do this together." Now, I can wrap my arms around her in a span of one deep, cleansing breath.

Why do I tell you this little anecdote?

To illustrate that the reasons we hold our voices close to our chest—or keep it solely to ourselves—can be anything. For me, I was told at that moment not to succumb to my fears and not to express my very real emotions. I had to be a "good little soldier" as my military dad would say. That lesson has informed my performance throughout my life. When I fully remembered it, realizing that much of the details were provided by my siblings, I realized that I could break free from one set of shackles that I let hold me back.

The Power of the Breath

That deep breath. I learned to breathe deeply in a moment of distress. It's been a godsend.

Taking a moment, even just the span of that deep breath, moves your thinking from the fight-flight-freeze area of your brain to a more logical, deliberate area. It also allows your brain to catch up to your mouth—you can think before you speak.

For example, tell me if this happened to you. You are at a company party. Your colleagues, friends, and boss are part of a group discussion on current events. They're laughing about something. You look down at your drink and hope no one looks your way. Deep inside, you think, "Where can I hide? What do you have to offer in this conversation? Nothing! Right?"

Fast forward; you've left the party and completed your commute home. As you pull out your keys to unlock your front door, the perfect comeback—a splendiferously funny retort—pops into your head. "Why couldn't I think of that?" you exclaim out loud.

Welcome to the largest club in the universe! The "*why-couldn't-I-think-of-that*" club.

The very idea of speaking up conjures up such debilitating fears. For me, I become that little girl cowering behind her mother. Even though today, I'd love to see an alien robot maid! How often have you heard that folks fear public speaking more than death or taxes? I, however, think the biggest is fear of speaking up.

The very idea of speaking up can conjure up whatever deep-seated fears you may have. These can cripple you. First, your throat goes dry and tightens. Your eyes start to bug out with fear and you hope no one notices as you begin to perspire (at least in my experience).

Guess what? No one sees your discomfort. They are too busy getting caught up in their own fears. Yep, we all have them.

Then something magical happens. A tiny quiet voice hidden in the deepest regions of your mind whispers, "All you need to do is take a deep breath." Can you believe it? It's that simple. That's the magic moment. That deep relaxing breath takes you out of the fear zone and into the "I can do it" zone.

It takes practice, though.

I had a stress management coach suggested a practice reminder to help me make deep breathing "a thing." Every time I drove to a stoplight or stop sign, she told me to take three deep breaths. I was resistant in those days, to say the least. After a week though, I was amazed. I was on the highway and a car sped up in the lane next to me, then immediately cut over into my lane. My usual response would have bordered on a vocal road rage with a large helping of horn pounding. This time, however, I remember saying out loud, to my son who was sitting next to me, "Well, he obviously needs to get somewhere ten seconds faster." My son laughed and my ire dissipated. That, to me, was a turning point. Practice actually pays off.

Now I'm Breathing. What Next?

Once you gain that breathing skill—which will lead to that grace-under-pressure skill as well—you begin to tell your story. Our voice comes through in many ways: how you phrase things, stories you tell, the innate level of self-esteem, confidence. It also is reflected in how we present ourselves, whether in writing, speaking, or even participating in activities.

I tell you, after spending many years training executives on how to develop a message, work with the media, deliver speeches, and manage large internal presentations, I thought I had this public speaking and voice under control. I've authored books that were sent to the President—yes, that one. I've published articles in major magazines as a corporate ghostwriter. I authored speeches delivered by CEOs. Yep. I had a voice down.

It just wasn't my voice.

In my profession, I worked to help others share their voices. I once worked with a CEO who presented adequately by being very dry. I helped him to loosen up and show his passion for our burgeoning technology. We worked on telling stories to weave the facts through. We used those facts to add depth to the story instead of just reciting facts. I helped a company evangelist develop his comfort level in presenting information in an organized, off-the-cuff, and entertaining manner. We needed to build up his persuasive skills. I worked with my clients to discern where their level of comfort was and fashioned materials using their words and their voices to ensure the information was authentic and credible.

However, when it came to preparing myself—crickets. Instant dry throat. Instant fast heartbeat.

Then I sat down to write a chapter for an anthology and froze. I attempted a few blog posts and thought, *this can be better.* **I was my own worst critic. Who wants to hear from me? What do I have to say that anyone wants to hear? These questions that flooded my brain were instant brakes on any progress. Then I wondered. What's missing? It was simple. My voice.**

I was so adept at reflecting others' voices, I kept mine shut. I was a good writer, a great coach as long as I held onto my own opinions and let others shine. I was still that little girl hiding behind her mother's skirt. Only in real life, I was an experienced communications and media coach hiding behind a big portfolio of work. How in the heavens did I let this happen?

Easy.

We are so busy living life and maintaining a certain equilibrium, that we don't want to rock the boat. Fear and resistance work together to keep us from moving forward. Then, go figure. We get comfortable with the status quo. Who wants to change that? Yes, it keeps us from changing. That is not our natural state, though. The Greek philosopher Heraclitus said, "There is nothing permanent except change." That said, it takes bravery and vision, strength and grace to do what is needed. To take that first step to allow change in and to learn how to let it flow gracefully around you.

So what did I do? I joined a Toastmasters group. I began to speak on subjects that I found interesting. Not subjects my boss needed. Not subjects that interested my friends and colleagues. Me. Subjects and themes that interested me.

As I did this, I found a new kind of confidence. A confidence that didn't need a conference room and a PowerPoint slide to allow me to speak up. I experienced, in my Toastmasters group, an audience on the same path as I was on. A path to get better at public speaking, to find their voices, and to grow in their leadership skills too. It was liberating, in a sense. It was as powerful as those magical moments that cause us to breathe deeply.

That first step led to the next step. I wrote an ebook, *Three Magic Questions to Instantly Improve Your Communications.* Then I crossed the scariest bridge—I let a few folks *read* it! *Arrgh*! They could hate it. They could judge it. Or, as it happens, they could like it. They said they learned something.

Each speech I gave at Toastmasters bolstered my confidence. Each time I shared my ebook with someone, I felt proud. I've now participated in five best-selling anthologies. I've given regular talks on the power of effective communications. I've conducted several media training workshops. I now host a podcast, Cardiac Conversations, and head up a national non-profit.

That first recognition, for me, was that I had quieted my own voice to support others. Once I surmised I had the power to change, that change led me through an enlightening path.

Pulling It All Together

Remember those quiet moments when a flash of a memory comes through? I said these are precious and perceptive moments. So much of who we are are housed in those snippets. Those fragments give us clues to who we are at our core. **All it takes is a little time—add a drop of attention and a dollop of change—and voila! Your voice will shine through loud and clear. Here are a few "news you can use" tips to start your journey:**

1. ***Simply Remember and Recast***
   We all have a voice, a story to tell. Each of us is here for that reason: to tell our stories. As I relate in my Rosie the Robot experience, sometimes stories that drive your life may not be solely owned by you. The first step in finding and defining your voice is to take inventory of your vignettes—those memory-based stories that run through your mind and subconsciously define you. Are they your stories? Did you hear them from a loved one from their perspective? Can you redefine them from your perspective? Remember how I meditated on that little girl and offered my adult hand to support her? This step helps you to redefine your own memories to reflect who you are at your very core.

2. ***Breathe Life Into Your Voice***
   Breath is the essence of our spirit. By adopting a practice to remember to breathe deeply allows you to build a new skill. One that moves you gracefully, and sometimes imperceptibly, out of the stress-filled fight-flight-freeze state to the more deliberate, logical state. It allows you to take a nanosecond to let your mind catch up and listen to your inner guidance.

3. ***Jump In!***
   Take a first step in letting your inner voice shine through. Whether it's a big step or a little one doesn't matter. What matters is that it's a step. Mine was establishing a few blog posts, stumbling a little, and finding

Toastmasters. Yours may be completely different, but it's an important step.

British author Neil Gaiman said it best. He said, "The one thing that you have that nobody else has is you. Your voice, your mind, your story, your vision. So, write and draw and build and play and dance and live as only you can."

I can't wait to hear your voice!

Jeanne Alford

An experienced speaker, trainer, writer, and PR expert, Jeanne Alford spent her career honing her expertise in communications. She has directed national and international public affairs and public relations programs for several brands including Dolby, Philips Electronics, and Visa. She has also worked with leaders at some of the most innovative startups in Silicon Valley. No matter what position she held, her focus remains on telling a compelling branding story.

Jeanne's communications and PR campaigns have changed media perceptions, garnered national and international awareness for issues, and helped to strongly position executives as industry leaders. As an advocate for employee communications and crisis communications, she led programs to ensure that a company's most important asset, its people, are kept informed. As a trainer, she has assisted many executives in refining and leveraging their media efforts to ensure their company story is told through the eyes of respected media writers and broadcasters.

Today, Jeanne works with individuals and small businesses to tell their most captivating stories—in the media, with customers, and among their colleagues. As a communications and media coach, she strives to apply those skills so her clients can tell their best stories using the most effective platforms. Her focus is on developing communications strategies and coaching business leaders to elevate and refine their message.

Jeanne, a best-selling co-author and writer, published several business articles, white papers, and marketing campaigns. Her materials have appeared in daily newspapers, national business publications, and on several online sites. She most recently authored "3 Magic Questions to Instantly Improve Your Communications," which is available to download at BeClear101.com.

Email: jeanne@alfordcommunications.com
Phone: 415-971-3344
Websites: alfordcommunications.com, beclear101.com
Facebook: https://www.facebook.com/BeClear101-1896566077223594/
LinkedIn: https://www.linkedin.com/in/jeannealford
Twitter: @jealford

SOAR THE COSMOS WITHIN AND FLY THE GALAXIES WITHOUT

BY KARINA ARAGON

As I sit here in a dark candle lit room, deep in thought, putting structure to my rapid mind, I begin to record every word. Gathering the multiple streams of information and attempting to organize them as I begin to write my first chapter of my first published book. I ask myself, how will I condense my wise information into understandable, practical advice for anyone who may need it. I think about many stories that I can tell about breaking free and stepping into my power, this being one of them. This is a new time, a new age, and it's a new world. For the sake of space I will use NW for new world and OW for old world. We're leaving behind an OW and stepping collectively into a NW.

The NW is one that is foreign and new to all of us. Everything is unpredictable, constantly changing and evolving at increasing rates, whether that is the apps on our phones, the global changes in weather, or the changes in the systems and structures. We all are evolving together and learning who we are in this constantly changing NW. This could be unsettling for most, especially those of the OW and those of us that are in-between worlds such as myself, we are the Xennials. We are hybrids, which means we had an analog childhood and a digital adulthood. We were taught and raised in the OW giving us the necessary tools to survive there. However, we were not given the tools to survive in the NW and we are learning them along the way in our adult lives. Being a Xennial is a big responsibility; essentially we act as the bridge between the worlds and generations. We teach the younger generations how to survive in the OW and we show the older generations the tools necessary to survive in the NW.

Okay, so I got a little off track but I want to bring you back. So you're probably wondering what in the galaxies I'm doing sitting in a dark candle lit room? *My power is out from all the solar winds and California fires; the state of California announced a state of emergency. My challenge today was my hometown got evacuated on the day I had allotted to write this first draft.* The morning that was supposed to be filled with creativity and writing ended up being a morning of panic and packing not knowing if I would ever see my home again. This was an obstacle that I had to overcome by using my battery-operated voice recorder where I recorded most of what I'm writing to you right now. Rewind to last year when I was contemplating being in this book, it all started with my solar return on August 12, 2019. Twelve days after my solar return (aka my birthday) my dog Ted passed away. I noticed many people reported on social media of their pets dying also. This sent me into reaching a little more into the cosmos; I found that Saturn was exactly opposite the "Dog Star", which is Sirius, the brightest star in the night sky along with the Mars and Venus conjunction. Not only that but we have had back-to-back geomagnetic storms, which I think is partially due to the increase of the sun's coronal hole.

Scientists have observed many new findings including neutron star collisions, black hole mergers, and new celestial bodies. Earth is also experiencing some new global weather shifts, systems merging, and new technologies. Humanity is also undergoing symptoms of integration of all these changes including our animals.

"AS ABOVE SO BELOW"

Anyways, the death of my dog was unexpected and everything changed in my daily routines. I was lost and confused which led to a decrease in my social media presence on YouTube, Facebook, and Instagram, as well as reconsidering participating in this book. I took a break and allowed myself to have the much-needed downtime to process my loss and to figure out where I'm being guided to next. I decided that it was this book that I needed to do. Yes, it was a time when I felt very alone and lost, but for some reason I felt as though this is what the universe really wanted for me next. **The first step is the most important: it is having the courage to take that first step toward the greatness that God has for you.**

When a baby is learning to walk it doesn't think about where it's going to go when it finally learns to walk or run. It focuses on that moment and the act of taking its first step, which its guardian is trying to encourage. We too have guardians, just as a child does, that are guiding and nudging us to learn. The universe guides us along our soul's path. We sometimes get held back in the first step because we are thinking of where we will go next. **My advice would be to take the step, be in the moment every day, and your path will develop and become more illuminated.** Sometimes it's about making it up as you go along; that's what keeps life so interesting.

"CHALLENGES ARE WHAT MAKE LIFE INTERESTING AND OVERCOMING THEM IS WHAT MAKES LIFE MEANINGFUL"

We all are trying to purge the past old world and step into the new world. We are in search of balance internally and externally and we are finding ways to help assist one another in finding that happy medium in sustainability and structure. When I was younger I found my stability and structure around playing pool. When I was seven I started playing pool. I joined my first pool league at twenty-one and by thirty-two I was playing nationals in Vegas.

There was a point in my life when I decided it was time to step out of my shell and be heard. After all I've done a lot of self-discovery, education, and investments in myself, why not? When I was a child I felt like I didn't have a voice, the trauma silenced me but there was a smart enlightened old soul wanting to be expressed. I was the firstborn so naturally I was surrounded by a bunch of adults not having siblings for the first decade of my existence. My nineteen-year-old mother birthed me into her childhood home where I spent my toddler years being raised with my grandparents.

When I was a kid my papa would put a mattress out on the balcony and he would point out all the constellations, I was always intrigued and inspired by the stories he would tell, much more interested in the nocturnal sky then learning to speak Spanish, which you can assume drove him nuts. My papa had a big influence on my life; he taught me how to play pool and box. In short my mom married a substance-abused husband and had a few more kids. Back and forth I walked from my house to my home since we lived a block from my grandparents. There was a field that gave me an accessed shortcut to my grandparents' house where I would take my sister to escape when things got bad at the house. It seemed as though I was always in the midst of their turbulent relationship, finding no peace at my house. Whenever it was time to leave after a visit with my grandparents, I would hide inside the pool table not to be found until my mom gave up and left. They never found my hiding spot after all those years.

Fast forward. I got kicked out at the age of fifteen and went to live-in nanny for my aunt. After a year, I moved back with my grandparents. I respected them very much and they wanted me to go to college, which led to my degree in psychology today.

I decided to create new family cycles and I was the first college graduate in my family. I studied theater at DVC, transferred to UCSD, enjoyed working the productions at the La Jolla Playhouse, and graduated with my degree in Psychology at CSUEB.

Through all this I was battling the same type of relationships my mom had, until one day I got the perspective and strength to get out and free myself from the generational curse. It was that one exhausted morning in San Diego after a big fight with my boyfriend the prior night. I watched the sun come up and my puffy eyes peered above into the dawn skies watching the birds fly by singing their songs. As I meditated on the sounds I realized they were mockingbirds making the sounds of car alarms. This lifted my spirits with laughter as their message was revealed. These birds were singing something that they had learned in their environment growing up, which obviously was not their own song. We have models that teach us their songs just like the cars were teaching the birds. The mockingbirds' song was a parody of my song. I saw abuse in my childhood environment, which has been paired with love and relationships. I sat there in deep thought thinking about how angry I've been with my mother for not protecting me as a child. However, now is a different story; it's my story, not my mom's anymore. I realized I have control of whom I allow into my life, for I am a grown adult and it's not her job to protect me anymore, it's mine. **This was my aha moment which led to an important turning point of taking my control back.**

"SELF CARE IS HOW YOU TAKE YOUR POWER BACK."

I grabbed a picture of myself as a child and as I looked at it I thought, *I need to protect her. I can't blame my mom anymore; now I have a choice, and I choose to take my power back and do what my mom didn't.* **My epiphany came from the aha moment with the mockingbirds and it is this: if I continue down this road I know where it leads,** I've seen it, and I will be mad at myself like I have been with my mother. Once you have an awakening like this you cannot go back, because something so deep in the unconscious has now surfaced into the conscious mind. When this happens that thing no longer has control over you because it's no longer in the dark (unconscious), it is in the known revealed by the light (consciousness). With that being said that very week while in San Diego I ended that relationship; that was one of the hardest things I've ever had to do. We were both better off for the decision I chose to make. I was taught from a young age that it was okay for people to abuse, disrespect, take advantage, and overstep my boundaries. I naturally fell into similar relationships and partnerships with people that mirror these not-so-great "role model" qualities. This influenced my romantic relationships and friendships. Low self-worth and codependency was environmentally learned in childhood. From being a caregiver to my mother, siblings, and other family, I was attracted to people that also needed this kind of caregiving.

What sets a successful person with the same upbringing apart is what they choose. You have a choice every day! I challenge you to make a conscious choice to be different than what you were taught. Not only was I the first college graduate in my family, but I also broke karmic cycles of abuse and early motherhood. **Now, I'm taking these hardships and making them a tool for success to help others that share a similar story. I help and teach others how to break free and step into their own power like I have done.** *After the big break up, I finished out my semester of school needing some stability after losing my job and my car breaking down.* I took some much-needed time to heal and make some money. I finally had enough money so I bought myself my first car and signed back up for college. *Mid quarter I got a phone call that you never want to get; my brother was diagnosed with cancer. It was very challenging to focus when all I wanted was to be up north with my family.* I stuck it out and I got the best grades that quarter. I chose to channel my sadness and fear into fuel for my studies. My brother fought the good fight and not too long after,

I received my diploma. I never gave up on my education, no matter what obstacles got in my way, and I will never give up on myself either.

"REACH FOR YOUR DREAMS DON'T LET YOUR DAILY CHORES AND HURDLES KEEP YOU FROM REACHING THEM."

After I graduated I bought myself a vacation to Thailand and Nepal. When I returned I made a conscious choice to live alone, to go inward, and start my healing journey to self-actualization. I desired to have a healthy relationship and I would eventually want to share my life with my best friend. I understood I needed to live alone for once in my life and commit to myself first before I was able to commit to anyone else.

I began my own personal journey and one day while enjoying my new space I came across an article that said that people with a certain moon placement in their natal birth chart could be miss diagnosed as bipolar. This sparked my interest for many reasons. I naturally wanted to know more and I started studying astrology. I began to see patterns and trends with the people in my life. Not only that, I started to learn more about myself on an objective level. The science of the human mind, the study of nature versus nurture and environmental factors all had an effect on human behavior and now the external astronomical bodies? This sent me into a rabbit hole of research. Back in 2011 Psychology Today wrote an article finding that scientists found a statistical significance between personality and time of year you were born. I mean if disease levels, personal disorders, diet and activity levels all vary with seasons, why not personality? I've been studying and researching ever since and now I'm hosting my own classes and workshops.

"WHEN YOU CHANGE THE THINGS YOU LOOK AT THE THINGS YOU LOOK AT CHANGE." (DR. WAYNE DYER)

Don't let any of your childhood and life experiences go to waste. Before my self-actualization I felt alone but now I feel emotionally independent. I'm ready to step out into my power as the universe prepared for me, to help others, and share my story and the tools I've learned along the way, whether that be healing through your birth chart, acting on your own stage, or just playing a confident game of pool.

Key Takeaways To Stepping Into Your Power

- The first step is the most important; it is having the courage to take that first step toward the greatness that God has for you.
- My advice would be to take the step, be in the moment every day, and your path will develop and become more illuminated.
- Listen for the aha moment which is the powerful turning point of taking your control back. My epiphany came from the aha moment with the mockingbirds and it is this: if I continue down this road I know where it leads.
- What sets a successful person with the same upbringing apart is what they choose. You have a choice every day!
- Now take your hardships and make them a tool for success to help others that share a similar story. Help and teach others how to break free and stand in their own power.

"WHAT COULD YOU DO TOMORROW, THAT YOU DIDN'T DO YESTERDAY, THAT WOULD GET YOUR GOALS CLOSER THAN THEY WERE TODAY?" (KARINA ARAGON)

Karina Aragon

She has been an entrepreneur for over ten years. Karina built a housekeeping and organizing business as an avenue of independence in her early years; this being one of her first creations, another form of being of service for others in their times of transformation.

She uses her magic hands to heal and assist others. Life coaching is her passion with focus in astrology and transformation, alternative medicine and health, as well as healing through the arts.

She uses a three-step process while helping and working with her clients. First she pulls the clients astrology birth chart which assesses the galactic cosmos to get acquainted with her clients souls DNA which accelerates the healing and coaching process. Secondly, it's time for talk therapy, which assists in identifying any root issues or obstacles that may be getting in the way of the client's growth. Lastly, she works with them to develop their goals and assist the client to map out a plan of accomplishment in reaching their soul's divine purpose and goals.

Karina's current goal is to write her first book by 2025 and to make a difference in the communities around the world through inspirational speaking about building the new world and teaching practical ways to use predictive astrology.

"Let's evolve and heal the collective one person at a time. We may not be able to reach everyone all at once but if we make a difference in one person's life and our direct communities, we will expand and make changes on a bigger scale."

Social Media Links
Email Address: LucidLivingLeoQueen@gmail.com
Phone Number: 510-691-3611
Website: LucidLivingMovement.com
Facebook page(s): https://www.facebook.com/LucidLivingMovement/
Twitter handle: https://twitter.com/KLA_LucidLiving
YouTube Channel:
http://www.youtube.com/c/KarinaAragonYourLucidLivingCoach
Instagram: @LucidLIvingCoach
WordPress: @LucidLivingCoach
LinkedIn: www.linkedin.com/in/KarinaAragonYourLucidLivingCoach

EMBRACE THE JOURNEY
BY LISA FAIRCHILD

I believe that each of us came into this world with gifts, talents, and a purpose. Then life happens and we lose our way. The thing is, I think that's how it's supposed to be. I believe we were born into life with a blueprint that is uniquely ours. As we experience situations and events in our life, we're faced with challenges and obstacles, some of which cause us to lose our way. If we look and if we're open these challenges can show us who we are, and can highlight our creativity, intuition, and resilience. This pattern is repeated throughout our lives. In effort to get along, belong, or simply to survive, we give ourselves away, back down from who we are or become what we believe others want or need us to be. It's when we recognize the discomfort in a misalignment for us that we can find our way back home.

Today's problems were yesterday's solutions. That fits with my beliefs. I believe our work is all about finding ourselves again and again. Standing in our power requires that we know who we are and what is ours. It's letting go of or shedding beliefs and habits of behavior that we took on in order to get by, to fit in, or to create order in what can sometimes feel like rocky terrain. Breaking free of the hold or pulls of external forces is not a one-shot deal. Life doesn't work that way. As we walk this journey, traverse the landscape of life we are faced with challenges, adversity and opportunity, perhaps a million chances to lose ourselves to find ourselves once more.

I know this about myself. I am and have always been wise, intuitive, and meant to heal and bridge relationships. I haven't always recognized and still don't always honor those gifts. In fact, what's required **for me to stand in my power is really the work of uncovering and recovering what was always mine to have and hold;** what was always mine to give and to recognize and address the situations, events, and emotions that move me into or out of myself.

There have been many events or happenings in my life that shaken me and woken me up to parts of myself that have been hidden, misused, or thrown me off center. I'd like to share three that stand out as being transformational in my life, where I discovered how to stand in my truth and my power.

The first one happened about ten years ago. I had gotten divorced several years earlier and was trying to find my new normal. During a networking meeting, I met a woman named Margaret who had a side business of reading handprints known as hand analysis. In case you've never heard of such (I hadn't), it's a little different from palm reading. Hand analysis is done by looking at both our physical hands but also our inked handprints. Our fingerprints are formed when we're in the womb and are unalterable. They tell us what our soul wants to experience as well as the lessons and challenges that are likely to come our way as our soul lives out its purpose. The lines on our hands, such as the heart, life, and headlines, as well as other markings can reveal some of our talents, gifts, and strengths.

As my inked handprints and my fingertips were examined through a magnifying glass, Margaret shared lots of information about what my hands had to say, but one thing stuck out for me. She told me that I was meant to be a leader and that somehow or for some reason, I had abandoned that part of myself. I immediately recognized it as the truth, so much so that I cried.

When I was a young girl, my family had a successful business, one that was a major employer in our community. Most of my classmates' parents worked for my family. The business provided for us in so many ways, but it also left me feeling isolated and different. While I was popular, I felt like it was the association with my family business, not me that people liked. We lived out of town which meant I didn't have the connections with friends that others who lived in the neighborhoods did. I felt the separation. My grandparents took us to school shopping in Palo Alto. We came home with nice, well-made clothing but it was different than the clothes my friends wore. I longed to have the bright pink furry peacoat that all my friends had because I so wanted to fit in and to belong. Hearing Margaret's comment that I had shut down my leader, I understood and recognized for the first time that I had made a decision long ago to hold back a part of myself because it would further call attention to how I was different when all I wanted to do was fit in.

My tears also reflected the knowledge that I could now free myself of that story. In the preceding months I had seen in my mind's eye myself being a leader, being on stage, having a message but none of it made sense to me at the time. I recognized that it was no longer necessary for me to hide that part of myself. I wasn't sure whether reading handprints had any real truths, but I recognized the truth in myself and consciously made the choice to step into and begin to own the leader inside of me.

The next shake up, wake up in my life happened when I decided to step away from my religion. I was born and raised Catholic. I had fallen away from religion as a young adult but had returned to the church after having my son. However, it was after my divorce that I became even more involved in the church, in fact, where I began to use *my leader* that I had hidden for years. I facilitated a divorced-and-separated group; I was chair of the spiritual life committee and even chair of the parish council. I loved what I was doing, and I loved being part of the community. As my role got bigger and I became more visible, I began to feel an internal gnawing—something was out of sort and out of balance within myself. I was good with God, but less good with the church as an institution. I was at odds and not living congruent with some of the church teachings. I felt hypocritical holding the positions I held at church given my personal convictions. This incongruence along with some changes that were taking place at my church finally reached its tipping point and I made the decision to step down from my roles and leave the church. It was a hard decision for me and one that I took very seriously. My faith was important to me and much of my social life was built at and around my church community. Many of my friendships ended because of my decision. It was a very painful time in my life. I didn't expect or understand how friendships could be lost in the context of religion. I tried hard to save them, but very few survived. There were moments I thought about going back so that I could keep my friends, but I knew that as uncomfortable as it was to feel alone, it was more uncomfortable to be at out of alignment with myself. I chose me. I fine-tuned my definition, care, and feeding of my relationships and began the process of rebuilding new friendships.

My most recent come-to-Jesus with myself happened just a few months ago. I've been keeping a journal for years—a literal history of my thoughts, mistakes, lessons, blessings, and joys that have transpired over the years.

One day as I wrote in my journal, I realized that I have been repeating and recycling the same stories for years—in fact, most of my life. Yes, the context had changed several times but there was a thread of sameness to it. **It was an old story that didn't have a good ending and I was sick of telling it. It was The Story of Almost.** It went like this: I'm *almost* successful, *almost* the weight I want to be. I *almost* finished what I started and *almost* have the life I want. In other words, I kept complaining or bemoaning the same things over and over. Sadly, even some of my relationships were also written into The Story of Almost.

This realization (at age sixty-two) hit me like a ton of bricks. What needed to change in my life? I needed to *end* this story and begin to craft a new story of joy, love, and authenticity.

The Story of Almost didn't mean I've had a life of hardship; in fact, for the most part, the opposite is true. Yes, there's been bumps, but I've had a blessed life. Rather it is about me owning and sharing the gifts and talents I was given. The blueprint I spoke of earlier. We all have gifts and talents that are uniquely ours and I believe we are meant to share them. For reasons that perhaps made sense at one time, I've hidden or been afraid of using many of mine. I know why I did this, but that too is a story that no longer serves me. Yesterday's solutions are often today's problems and I'm now culling what no longer fits. I'm creating the space for new, better, bolder!

Crafting a new story is a two-pronged effort: a start and a stop. It requires a vow of persistence, consistency, and rigorous honesty. The start prong is to steadfastly commit to some new daily practices that push me to do more, to *be* more, and to bust through my beliefs about what's possible.

The second prong is clearing out and making space for new and different realities. **I know that if I want to be different, I have to *be* and *do* different.** I'm carefully examining my stories and beliefs, asking myself, "Does this serve me? Does it bring me joy?" If the answer is no, then I'm letting it go!

I'm dreaming *big*, asking myself, "What do I want?" and then drilling down into my answers to get as specific as possible. I'm listening to my heart untethered from the past. **The Story Of Almost is now closed for business.**

The new story is being written day by day. I don't know all the pieces or how it will play out but I know this: it's a story of joy, love, and authenticity. It is, and will be, a celebration of who I am. **I will be imperfect, vulnerable, and have fun putting myself out there and using my gifts. I am whole and complete while continuing to learn and grow.** I'm free to be *me*! It feels wonderful!

What does it take to stand in our power? It takes courage! Courage to notice, courage to feel the emotions—the love, hate, anger, and disappointment. I often get pretty banged up emotionally before I pay attention to life's lessons and opportunities, but I'm getting better. I now recognize the pain points in my life as the sign that something is supposed to be happening and to dive in willingly.

I think we do ourselves injustice when we avoid doing something different so that we can change our circumstances. **We tell ourselves that change is hard.** It's a lie we tell ourselves that keeps us small. We forget that we wouldn't be considering changing ourselves or our circumstances, if what we were currently being or doing was working. **Change is not a hard or easy proposition. Changing or not changing are both hard.** One hard thing is what we've known and done in the past. We know the outcome. The other hard is unknown, unfamiliar and therefore uncomfortable. But that second hard, the hard that comes with change also holds the hope and the promise for a new beginning and better outcome.

This is what I know for sure. The tension and messy parts of our life are there to teach us, to usher us into being. I believe that whether they come gently, or they take us to our knees, the adversities in life is an invitation for our soul to wake up. If you've lost yourself and it's time to get back home, wake up my friend and embrace the journey.

Tips to Being Yourself

1. Be willing to embrace the journey.
2. Explore and discover your gifts and talents. They are your superpower.
3. Speak your truth, dream big and choose to write your own story.
4. Catch and release what no longer serves you.
5. Embrace change as it comes.
6. Let any discomfort be your GPS to find your way back home to yourself.

Lisa Fairchild

Lisa Fairchild is a life coach, public speaker, and workshop facilitator. Her work is focused on relationships—the relationships we have with people, and the ones we have with the events and situations in our lives. The heart of her work is helping people tap into their inner wisdom and to honor and trust themselves as the expert on their lives. She believes that when we recognize and live from our *most*—our truest, most authentic self—and bring that into all aspects of our relationships and life, we feel aligned, congruent, and joyful. Her clients describe her as intuitive, insightful, and supportive. Clients feel focused, resourceful, and empowered to address the choices and decisions in their relationships and lives.

Lisa started coaching in 2007 after over a twenty-year career in Human Resources. She has a BA in Business Administration and an MBA in Human Resources. She received her coaching education through Coach Inc. and is a member of the International Coach Federation. She is a trained Points-Of-You® practitioner and uses the tools in her coaching and in personal and professional development workshops.

Lisa is committed to life-long learning and is always seeking new opportunities that support personal and professional growth, create adventure, and bring fulfillment.

https://www.linkedin.com/in/lisafairchildcoach/
https://www.instagram.com/ontheedgeofcoaching_lisa/
https://www.facebook.com/lisa.fairchild.58
https://www.facebook.com/On-The-Edge-Of-Coaching-150190520778/

SECTION 3:

Discover Your Greatness

AWAKEN YOUR GREATNESS
BY MARY THOMAS, MD

It had been a very long time.

Forty-six years to be exact, that I held this deep desire within me to do this *one* thing.

The year was 1973. I was thirteen. A Legion of Mary member. Forcefully placed there.

That Saturday morning, as I dragged myself out of bed, would be a day that would change my course, my track. I was assigned to the local hospital. Bed 52, Medical Ward 3. Patient: Peggy Lim, seventy-four. Read the day's Gospel to patient. Sigh! I was still groggy from lack of sleep and sheer laziness.

Grabbed my Bible, put it into my satchel, and off I went searching for Peggy Lim.

Found her. She seemed drugged, in her own reverie. I tried to ask how she was. I heard a mumbling. Incoherent.

I settled down on the stool by her bed and fumbled. What was today's Gospel? Who would even know that? I am not a nun.

I decided to choose a passage myself. Psalm 23. "The Lord is my shepherd . . ." I thought that should be suitable. She needed a shepherd right now, I figured.

I began reading it. Slowly. No response. Could she even hear me? I went closer. I read again. No response. *Oh! Has she died?* I tried again. No response. *Oh no! This can't happen.* No! I looked around. There were two rows of beds, all of which had women of all ages and conditions. Those ladies in white, yes, they are nurses. I ran to one of them.

"That lady, bed 52, is not moving! Died?"

"What?!" the lady in white snapped.

Goodness, what am I supposed to say then?

"What are you doing here? Children are not allowed in the wards!"

Children? Did I look like a five-year old?! I was a tall thirteen-year old.

This was not working. I looked around. Saw a gentleman in a long, white coat. Yes, I know that one. He is a doctor. Ran to him. Told him that the lady in bed 52 was not moving. He listened to me. Yes, he actually did! He said something to the nurses and ran over to bed 52. All of them crowded around the bed. I could only peer through, in between them. The man in the coat was giving instructions, everyone listening and rushing across the room to follow those instructions. In less than ten minutes, Peggy Lim was moving again. There were wires strapped to her, but never mind, she was actually moving, her eyes half-open. I just stared at Mr. White Long Coat in awe. Wow! He knew what to do to bring back the dead! Wow! That's just wow! What was that? What did he do? How did he know what to do?

I could not continue my assignment for the day, but I had a new assignment; it "bore" (for want of a better word) right through me. It was an ignition, some sort of fire, and if you ask me today, I still don't know how to describe it.

And hence started my journey, which I completed forty-six years later.

In sharing my journey, I would say there are some facts that remain unchanged. We hear it *all* the time. We hear it *repeatedly*. They are *timeless*. And there lies the *truth*. There are simply no two ways about it.

You must have a *burning* desire.

Many of us do not even know that we actually *have* a burning desire. That desire that was ignited decades ago, but now is in embers, buried somewhere. But know one thing: they are embers waiting to be *reignited*. I really did not know that there was this deep desire. I knew I was awestruck that day. I knew it "hit" me hard, but I didn't know it would subconsciously rear its head often. When I was to choose my undergraduate course, inevitably I chose medicine. It was my father who said "no." (I had to listen to my sponsor.) If I had to write an essay or composition, I would always choose to write about diseases or doctors. If I were chosen to do a play, I would be taking the part of the "doctor." The books and magazines I bought, borrowed, and read; the programs I watched; the groups I joined were always in some way connected to health care. The NGOs that my peers and I pioneered were all healthcare-based. And these were all happening by default. It was not a conscious effort or planned. My life circled around anything to do with health and healthcare. I would find my way there. Literally, gravitate toward it. Later, many years later, when I discovered the Law of Attraction, I realized that the "embers in my soul" were attracting these situations to me. It was these "embers" again that brought me to the dean's office of my alma mater, where I finally graduated with my medical degree.

So, reflect on it. Give yourself that what you owe yourself. Think back of what you subconsciously keep going back to. A certain situation, a consistent pattern that makes you happy. That's the direction of your dreams.

Age. This is so important . . . to *ignore*.

To start with, these numbers are often placed with importance. As important as your name. Who even decided that? Time was created by man. It simply gives semblance and order (read: control) to our lives. That's it. Period. It is in no way a true reflection of anything you can or cannot do. It is *us* who decide. It is us who create the limits. It is us who create weak knees, aching backs, hyperopic eyes. Metaphysically, every disease is created by our minds. It has been proven time and again. Mind over matter. Our belief systems. Our conditioning. Our limited paradigms.

In medical school, I was in a class of 473 students. They were all decades younger than me. In principle, I do not tell anyone my age. I do not celebrate birthdays. I do not believe in any of this.

When you want to achieve your desire, you *only* stay focused on your desire. Nothing else.

A belief in a higher power.

This may be a bone of contention. But I must add this, as my personal experience has proven time and again that a higher power exists. Whatever you may wish to call it, there is no denying it.

It is a spiritual consciousness, a divine hand, the higher good, a great love. It is all encompassing. It cannot be erased. It is innate. It is your *power*. To be manifested by you. No one can take this away. Not even you, actually. It is *there*. It rises when you call upon it. Like a phoenix rising from the ashes, it rises from the "embers in your soul." Those embers will reignite.

Those flames will change your life forever.

Your greatness is *awakened*.

Tips to awaken your greatness:

1. Have a burning desire.
2. Ignore age.
3. Believe in a higher power.

Mary Thomas

Mary Thomas, MD shares her journey that altered the course of her life. A life-evolving journey that proves anything is possible.

Going through medical school in her senior years, fulfilling a lifelong calling, she wants the world to know that *anyone* can be, do, and achieve whatever they set their mind to, at any age, in anything.

You are limitless. When you know you are limitless, the possibilities are endless, infinite.

She enlists how it can be done and how it can add immense value, bringing joy, fulfillment, and a deep sense of purpose, elevating one to their higher level of consciousness.

Mary's mission now as a doctor, is to change disease-care to health-care, one patient at a time.

Thus, her advocacy, patient empowerment.

She knows that this can transform lives, bringing a phenomenal difference to health care.

She is in addition, a firm believer of soul-consciousness, where humanity is rapidly evolving.

With a change in the collective, frontiers will expand beyond current limitations, breaking down barriers and other obsolete paradigms.

Together with Prajna Shakti (the Strength of Wisdom), she knows all things are possible

Social Media Links
Email Address: drmarythomas09@gmail.com
Phone number: +639085250623
Facebook: https://www.facebook.com/mary.thomas.92123015

FINANCIAL INDEPENDENCE FOR WOMEN
BY REENU CHERIAN

Growing up, life was simple and comfortable for me. I was truly blessed because I got most things that I needed and wished for. I have always seen my dad take care of everything outside the house including our finances while my mom stayed in her favorite place in the house—"the kitchen"—and took care of everything else in the family. All my parents wanted from me was to study hard, get good grades, get a job, get married, and settle down comfortably. **I was not taught to have big dreams or goals or how to handle money. I had no idea about how money worked and did not realize how hard people had to work for it, because I got everything easily.**

I felt that we were rich, but looking back, we were squarely in the middle class, but we could afford vacations, go to private school and private college. What I had not realized then, was that my family knew how to live within their budget, so we were always comfortable. They made several sacrifices in other areas that didn't affect us, so I was blissfully ignorant. Everyone in our circle of friends also lived within their means and so we all felt like we were rich and had more than enough for everything in life.

Many of us come to America as immigrants, or as descendants of those who came in prior generations, with dreams of getting a high-paying job, make lots of money, buy a nice house, give our kids the best education, and then finally enjoy our retirement in peace. Coming to the US after my marriage, I became a true example of the phrase "The apple doesn't fall far from the tree." **I followed my mom's footsteps and was happy taking care of my husband and the house.** My husband worked in the IT field and was making good money, but little did I realize that almost half of our pay went away in taxes, insurance, and medical expenses. **Taxes—that was a new term to me as I was brought up in the Middle East and we never had to pay taxes there and everyone had free medical services. Then someone told us about tax saving strategies like investing in a 401K and buying a house to get tax deductions and build up equity with low down payments. That was when we bought our first home.** First thing we looked for in a house was to see if the payment would be comfortable for us and then still have money left over for other things in life. **This meant we were subconsciously trying to live within our budget and also invested fully in the company's 401K plan. But this didn't stay that way beyond a few years.**

My husband has always been very entrepreneurial, and I supported him in whatever he wanted to do. He worked in some startups, and he was taking below-market income for many years, with some successes, some failures, and long stints with the hopes of a big payout. We started several businesses which included running a restaurant, a real estate business, an IT corporate training company, and an enterprise blockchain application infrastructure company.

Being in business together has its ups and downs. Working together toward one common goal is always exciting but if the business hits a crisis, it affects us as a family. We hit those brick walls multiple times, whether it was losing the lease on the restaurant due to a change of building ownership, or having to lay off most of the fifty people in the training company because of challenges with our largest client, or getting stuck with bad real estate in the 2008 aftermath or losing bulk of the value of the stocks in the private company when the public company that bought us went in to bankruptcy when the dotcom bubble burst and the paper millions vanished.

It was during one of those down times that we were introduced to a business with a financial education philosophy. As soon as I heard the word "finance," my mind went into shutdown mode. I convinced myself

that I would not understand it. But what made me take a closer look at this opportunity was when one of our friends passed away, his family had to move back to their home country and the friends had to do a GoFundMe campaign to help with funeral expenses. **That awakened me. That was when I realized that it was my responsibility and duty to learn and understand how money worked and how I could also manage our personal finances.**

My husband took care of all our finances perfectly until he ventured into the startup world. When he became busy running the companies, he was distracted by the challenges of being a small business owner, dealing with payroll and other customer emergencies, and was not able to monitor our personal finances very closely. **Since I did not understand finances, I did not understand the impact we had with the market downturns, until I realized how much money we had lost in our 401K and real estate portfolio.**

I decided to educate myself. I attended several classes, read several books and learnt how one could save on taxes, plan for retirement, the importance of having an insurance and estate plan in place and how one can create active and passive income during retirement. **I started sharing it with my friends and family and quickly realized that 90 percent of the women in my community did not understand finances and therefore did not want to talk about it. That had a big impact on me. I soon realized that my calling in life was to educate women on finances and to make sure that their families would be taken care of if something unexpected happened in their lives.** Then I became even more passionate about sharing these concepts to everyone I came across.

In 2017, we had hit rock bottom, but we had to learn to trust that God was taking care of us. It took some time, and quite a bit of spiritual and personal growth—thankfully, we had access to several mentors, coaches, pastors, clairvoyants, and other gifted people who showed up in our lives before the disaster hit, and gave us many hints and insights, in many ways, direct and indirect. Not that we listened immediately or acted right away -but we were open, and always listened, even if we took the advice in one ear and out the other and resisted the change. **We had to eat some humble pie and learn to trust God, that he had been the *one* who always provided, not our brilliance that gave us all those things. Once we completely surrendered, and threw up the white flag, things started slowly improving.** In my speeches, I often begin with, "I would like to thank my

Lord for showing me my purpose in life and for making me an instrument in securing the futures of many families and will pursue this cause for as long as I live." This comes from the heart as I had to experience this through my life's lessons.

Even though I was religious and believed in God, and had seen many miracles happen in my life, I had felt entitled and wasn't quite willing to accept things as they were happening. As a trained engineer, it took many passionate arguments with *God*, during my prayer time, and intercessions by many powerful souls including my mother, and a lot of soul searching, before we truly recognized our purpose, and decided that we are going to live a life that made a difference to people around us.

"Financial independence." I kept hearing this word a lot, but was not sure what it fully meant. I realized that it meant different things to different people. For some, it meant having the freedom of time and money to do anything they wanted, for others it meant going to a nice fancy restaurant and not having to look at the price side of the menu, while for others it meant to be worry-free about money and health challenges during retirement life. It was a fascinating concept. How many people in this country are able to achieve this "financial independence"? To achieve it, we must first understand that this is a personal decision we have to make, which will include a lot of sacrifices and discipline on our part. Once the mind is set, then you must act.

We had to unlearn some bad habits learnt over the prior two decades of living in America, and learn some new habits in our finances, in our faith, in our relationships, and our ability to trust. We discovered that everyone perceives things differently as they view the world through a different lens. We also learnt that there are some fundamental principles that are laws common to all.

No one ever plans to fail; we only fail to plan. Finances are not taught to us in our schools or colleges. We all go into debt very easily, but no one ever tells us how to get out of debt and that is why only 2 percent of the people in the high net worth group know how to create inter-generational wealth. For our money to grow we need to have time for our money to grow and a strong financial foundation, so the earlier you start planning, the faster you will have enough money generating money and set you free financially. Imagine the possibilities that open when you reach that stage.

You have to start saving early and develop a habit of paying yourself first. Start with whatever you can, say 5–10 percent, and work toward consistently saving 30–40 percent of your income. The concept of FIRE[1]—Financial Independence, Retire Early—has a lot of supporters, even if it can feel aggressive for many: The idea is that if you can save money early when you are younger, you have more flexibility in your life. Essentially, if we save 10 percent, it takes nine years to create one year's worth of expenses. If you save 50 percent, it takes one year to create one year worth of living expenses (assuming constant costs, and no earnings on savings). The rule of thumb is to save twenty-five times your annual expenses so that if you withdrew just 4 percent of your investment, you are only touching interests and dividends, not your principal. If you want to be super wealthy, we are talking financially free with inter-generational wealth, we should save 40 percent of our incomes. Grant Cardone is one of the people who are advocating this philosophy. Just think about it—if governments can insist on taking 40 percent or more for their needs, why not us? After all, we are the ones working for the money. Now, that means that we must learn to live on 20 percent of our incomes, which is a tough ask for most people, as they are used to living on 120 percent. This is how the rich get richer, and the middle class gets poorer. We are sold a dream of a better house, better car, more things that we buy on credit, with money we don't have, and we get surprised that our next generation is worse off than our parents were, and we are slipping down further and further. Getting there isn't easy, as the roads are full of advertisements and traps designed to take our money and attention away from us being aware of these is a starting point. Begin saving whatever you can, and as you master these concepts, keep increasing the number by 1 percent each time, and pretty soon you will be in a very different place from where you started.

It is indeed a game, and we should approach it that way, with the condition that we have only one life, unlike a video game or a movie where we can restart when the main character dies. We need to protect against contingencies, these include health challenges, loss of income, accident, death of a family member, divorce, and the silent thief, inflation which steadily reduces our purchasing power every year. The ones who set the rules of the game, write it for everyone, so that they can take advantage of it themselves. **In order to have a strong financial foundation, you need**

1. FIRE - Financial Independence, Retire Early - https://en.wikipedia.org/wiki/FIRE_movement

to always have a diversified portfolio that helps you plan for all the different stages of life.

1. ***Present***: Protect your life, your money from inflation, high taxes and health; plan for kid's college
2. ***Future***: Plan to have lifetime fixed income to cover your fixed expenses during retirement and have long-term care protection
3. ***Lifestyle***: Discretionary income that one can use for lifestyle changes
4. ***Emergency***: Plan to have six months of living expenses money saved
5. ***Asset protection***: Have an estate plan in place to protect your assets

The choices we make today will affect our future. We should never think that we have to wait and make more money to be able to save, because everyone can save something. Every dollar counts. Start saving small amounts at first and gradually increase that number to something that will make you a little uncomfortable or else you will not do this consistently. Here are a couple of ideas I share with my friends, especially the women.

1. ***Track your expenses:*** Understand where and how much you spend in each area of your life, how much you need to save for your future and see where you can make changes. I know someone who was spending monthly $400 on a gardener, $240 on Starbucks coffees, and $110 on cable TV that she hardly watched. We discussed options and reduced these three expenses from $750/month to $180/month, giving her access to $570 in savings per month. We don't realize where our money is going and that is why we need to breakdown all our expenses big and small.
2. ***Do not fear finances:*** Finances are simple and you can learn how to understand them. Learn how long does it take for your money to double (Rule of 72)[2], learn about tax now, tax-deferred, and tax-exempt options and have a well-diversified portfolio for yourself.
3. ***Pay off debt:*** Rule of 72 also works against us when we are carrying debt on our credit cards, mortgages, cars, etc. Ever wonder why the $2000

2. Rule of 72: Dividing 72 by the interest rate gives an approximate number of years for money to double, for common interest rates like 6,7,8, 9,12 etc. It is an approximation of the formula: t=ln(2)/ln(1=r/100) ~ 72/r, where t is the number of periods required, and r is the interest rate, Source: https://en.wikipedia.org/wiki/Rule_of_72

credit card balance barely shrinks even after paying for many years? It is because only the interest is being paid. We need to have a strategy to tackle this. Some pay off the smallest balance first, and then put that toward the next highest, and so on, until everything is paid off and you are debt-free. Other strategies are to pay off the highest APR or the highest payment first, whichever gets rid of those and creates more cashflow the fastest. Mortgages were considered to be a good debt in a market where housing prices increased dramatically. In markets where housing prices are stagnant or decreasing, it might be better to get rid of that debt by paying additional principal every month. A 4 percent mortgage interest reduced for certain is better than the uncertainty and possible loss of principal in the stock market, when the markets slowdown from what we are used to in the last decade.

4. ***Automobiles***: Cars are a depreciating asset, with an interest to be paid over a long term such as sixty months or seventy-two months. We buy a $35,000 car, pay over $40,000 including interest to have a vehicle that is worth $15,000 at most when we paid it off, and have to worry about repair costs, and may have to repeat the cycle again. Consider buying a vehicle that has gone through bulk of the depreciation to save money on this.
5. ***Become financially literate***: Make it a priority that you will learn as much as you can. Take up financial classes, read books that will teach you how to retire financially free.
6. ***Work with a financial advisor***: Work with someone who understands your needs and is willing to help you achieve your goals to become financially independent.

Achieving financial freedom is possible for everyone, if we all take the time and effort to plan and are willing to make the sacrifices.

We understand everyone's situation and needs are different. We have been able to help people reach their financial goals and can help you only if you are willing to learn and commit to working hard. **Success is not achieved overnight.** We all have to go through the ups and downs of life to get to our ultimate goals. It is like riding a roller coaster. It is not an easy ride but if you hang on and stay in it, and have a coach or a supporting environment, **I guarantee you that it will be truly rewarding, because the scenery from the top will be different and more beautiful than from the bottom. Hope to see you all at the top.**

Reenu Cherian

Reenu Cherian is a financial advisor considered very knowledgeable and helpful in tax-saving and retirement strategies. She owns and operates an independent insurance and financial services agency, helping women achieve financial security. She has a bachelor's in computer engineering from Manipal Institute of Technology.

After graduation, she got married and immigrated to the US. Although she spent a few years working in the technology field, she has always been an entrepreneur at heart. She worked with a network marketing company in the US and went overseas to build a successful team in India when they expanded into that market. Many years later, she decided to buy an Indian restaurant, which she ran for five years. Afterward, she joined her husband and ran the HR and recruiting department for their corporate learning and Development company focused on technology training where they were able to get thousands of women, minorities, and veterans into brand-new careers in information technology.

Later in life, she realized that there were a lot of people who needed a better understanding of how money works and went through ups and downs in life for lack of a proper financial education and planning. She became very passionate about sharing her knowledge about business and personal finances to her friends and family. She strongly believes that women should be able to take care of their finances and build a secure future, not only for their retirement, but also to build a lasting legacy and create inter-generational wealth. She is actively involved in her community and is currently the Vice President of Malayalee Association of Northern CA (MANCA), a large non-profit focused on the social needs of the Keralite community in Bay Area. She lives in Mountain House, California with her husband, son, and mom.

reenu.r.cherian@gmail.com
(925) 322-1365 (cell)

HOW TO FLY ABOVE THE DARK CLOUDS BY RENNU DHILLON

"Letting go means to come to the realization that some people are part of your history and not part of your destiny."
Steve Maraboli

In the past thirty years I have learned many important lessons which have helped me in my journey of self-discovery, but the singular one that I apply in my life every day—be it with family, friends, business associates, or clients—is that one has to know when to turn the page and move on to the next chapter. It is important to be able to let go of any toxicity and negativity that we encounter, and instead of holding on or playing the victim, we need to establish that we are responsible for how we are treated. **Everyone, regardless of their gender, must figure out their own worth, and head onto the journey to freedom and self-realization, creating their own destiny.**

Thirty-three years ago, in 1986, I arrived in this county (United States) to live the dream that every young Indian girl envisioned and envisions: a happy marriage, a beautiful family, and a successful career. After all I witnessed this in the hundreds of Bollywood movies I watched and was raised by parents who remain in love even today, celebrating sixty years of commitment. I was born and raised in Kenya, Africa, by parents who were highly educated but most importantly believed in giving the best education to their children. I learned quickly to have a strong voice, to express my views without fear, and that my destiny was in my hands. My father, a very successful medical practitioner, community activist, and local politician, played a strong influence in my life to instill morals and values. I learned to speak my mind and grew up performing on stage and writing for various publications and newspapers expressing my strong—and many times controversial—views. **However, the one mistake I made was that I assumed everyone around me would have the same morals and values. Little did I know that the journey ahead would be a rude awakening to the realities of the world!**

Three days before a "fat Indian wedding" attended by hundreds in the small town of Mombasa, Kenya, my former in-laws showed their true colors by placing demands. Despite being educated and successful, their greed took over when they placed a price on their only son for his worth. The sad reality is that women are always given a lesser value despite being more educated than the groom. These demands were hidden from me and thankfully my parents stood firm but still ending up footing the bill for the groom's travel, accommodations, and unnecessary expenses for the family from Canada. This was just the beginning of several pathetic facades for the next four-and-a-half years, which included constantly "taunting" me for not getting their son's price to constant criticism that I was unable to bear a grandson for them.

I landed in the United States six days after the fat Indian wedding to learn that my so-called husband did not even own the several businesses he had claimed he did, and was married to another woman at the same time. I took the path of "this is my chosen destiny" to stick around for four years in an extremely abusive relationship, physically, mentally, and emotionally due to the fear of the Indian society, the fear of rejection, and dealing with the dramas of family and friends. I was always spiritual but turned even more so this direction when all doors seem to shut for me. During this horrific marriage, filled with infidelity, disrespect, and abuse, the one thing I acquired was some of the business acumen that my first husband had, since I left my career as a pharmacist to join the company we formed of developing food franchises.

During those four years with him, I played an instrumental part in growing the company which was snatched from me at the time of the divorce due to "separate property" evaluations. That is another horrific story in itself of the injustice in this country due to immigration laws applicable at that time to immigrants such as me.

November 21, 1991 is what I consider as the day I was reborn. I was served divorce papers which at that time I reluctantly accepted but now when I look back, I kick myself for doubting my own abilities to survive without a man. A problem with our Indian community is that societal traditions make us women feel so weak and incapable, placing undue pressure of conforming to what the society wants which includes staying in relationships that are not worth any consideration.

By now you are probably wondering that this is such a morbid story, why even finish reading it to the end. Well my dear reader friends, this is where the true journey begins. The most difficult part of a divorce is to accept that the other party has moved on, and in my case, moved on with my own employee. Betrayal had been twice: an employee and a spouse. Instead of crying, feeling the self-pity, living in regret, and shedding unnecessary tears for unworthy humans, I learned to quickly cease to mourn what I thought I could have with him, and make the most of what was possible. **I learned quickly that where there is no trust or respect, there can be no love.** My journey was not going to be easy, but it was not going to be impossible either.

I have raised two beautiful daughters who have grown into amazing young ladies, and have successfully joined and run the family business, Genius Kids, with my present husband Gill, and myself. Their biological father, a confirmed alcoholic, lived his life based on only monetary values, unable to cement a healthy relationship with his daughters. Tragically he reached out to us in the eleventh hour of his passing but I am glad we were all able to have some closure to many unanswered questions for thirty years. Hence my point of being able to shed the baggage, forgive, and forget. I bless him every day for the two priceless assets I got, our two daughters.

Today my two daughters are my greatest strength. I learned that the success and failures of any relationship, the good times, the bad times, all lie within our own hands and are our responsibility solely. **I accepted that**

it is better to have your heart broken by the person leaving your life, than to have them stay and break you continually.

Using the experience that I had from my personal relationships, my successes, and my failures, combined with the strength to bring back my voice to speak without fear, the strong foundation of education, the unconditional love of my two daughters, and the love and friendship I soon discovered in my second and current husband, I used these tools to accomplish my own destiny and future.

I have enjoyed experiences in founding new ideas and businesses from skincare, dating matrimonial agencies, employment agencies, and for the last eighteen years, a renowned educational franchise for childcare. It has been hard work but extremely gratifying. Today, together with my personal journey, I have become the inspiration for men, women, and children. **I use my voice and words to share my journey to empower others to realize that bad relationships and experiences do not need to define you or your future**. Through your tears, you should be able to see the clear blue skies and the eternal stars. **I hope my readers will realize that if you want to fly, you have to give up the garbage that weighs you down. Courage is the first of our human qualities that guarantees our future.**

As women we need to remember that life is a journey filled with lessons, heartaches, joys and sorrows, hardships and special moments that will eventually lead us to our destination or purpose in life. This journey is not smooth, and for many, filled with turmoil. However, as Eleanor Roosevelt once said, "A woman is like a tea bag. You cannot tell how strong she is until you place her in hot water." Some women get lost in the fire while others rise above and build and change their future.

As women we need to remember that everyone's journey is not just about love, but it could be about purpose. **When I was young, I could not wait to grow up. Now at almost sixty, I realize that growing up never ends. To stay above and beyond the societal pressures and traditions, we must learn to fight for what we want**. It is as simple as that. I once read that if you live in your head for too long, you run the risk for becoming your own secret. Life is about experiencing new lessons every day and not about pondering in the past or dwelling on your mistakes.

I learned quickly from dealing with an unfaithful husband and selfish relatives that it is important to love yourself. It is important to rebuild yourself from every fall. Many times, we have to fall before we can rise and learn from the fall.

Hard work is not always an essential ingredient to one's success. Yes, we are all taught from a young age that if we work hard, everything will fall into place, but this is not always the reality of life. It is important to equip one's self with purpose, passion, commitment, and confidence. Using these tools, you can create your personal power and freedom of choice. **If you lack confidence and rely on others, you will probably keep finding excuses to stay in that negative environment and relationship, procrastinating out of fear.** I remember the words of Napoleon Hill: "Whatever the mind can conceive and believe, it can achieve."

Indian women are raised to keep doing things that can give others joy and fulfillment, and we forget that our own needs and purposes matter. The secret to your self-worth and happiness is to set aside your own desires and goals, and ensure that they align with your own unique purpose in life. Success, be it personal or professional, is not just a destination but a journey. Along this short journey we call life, your passions may shift or even disappear. In this journey, many passengers may jump on board to deter or delay the trip. Keep the steering wheel and direction of this journey in your hands. I read somewhere that knowing how to achieve success is like knowing the combination to a digital lock. If you miss any of the numbers the lock will not open. Keep the code to your digital lock in your hands, giving yourself the peace of mind that no one will steal your self-worth or confidence.

Being an entrepreneur means different things to different people. For me personally, entrepreneurialism means making a difference to someone every day, be it an adult, a child, a friend, or someone I have just met. Using my creative, positive energy, I am truly excited to be able to empower my staff who are primarily women of all ages to be able to achieve their dreams. **My three ingredients for success to all women would be to ensure that whatever you do, be sure that your values are aligned with the company you work for, as well as the friends you keep. Always have a role model to inspire and motivate you until you can be your own role model. Finally, be your own ambassador and strive to be better than what you are.**

As Madonna once said, "I'm tough, I'm ambitious, and I know exactly what I want. If that makes me a bitch, okay."

Tips to Help You Fly Above the Dark Clouds

1. Release what is holding you back
2. Be mindful about what you choose to believe in
3. Align your choices with your morals and values
4. Be willing to pursue your definition of success no matter what
5. Choose to fly and soar above the dark clouds, steering the direction of your own wings

Rennu Dhillon

Rennu Dhillon is the founder and CEO of Genius Kids, an award-winning early education franchise. Described as a "woman of many talents," a well-known Bay Area resident and community activist, emcee, and public speaker, Rennu has a Bachelor of Science (Hons), Pharmacy and Doctor of Science in Natural Sciences. She was born and raised in Kenya, East Africa and completed her education in England. She has made several contributions to news publications during her academic years and began writing poems and articles at age eight. Founder and CEO of Genius Kids, now a national franchise with over thirty-eight locations in California, and described as the "Harvard of Preschools," Rennu's inspirational story has been featured on worldwide documentaries to include CNNMoney.com, TV 5 Monde, KRON 4, SONY Asia TV, and Doordarshan India. She is a popular radio host of her weekly talk show, *Candid Conversations with Rennu Dhillon*, and is invited worldwide to speak on various issues affecting women and children, including the House of Lords, United Kingdom.

Rennu hopes to inspire every person who feels their life has fallen apart, to be able to steer the wheel in the direction of their dreams. Her focus at Genius Kids is to equip every child with the life skills for success.

@rennudhillon
https://www.facebook.com/rennu.dhillon
https://www.instagram.com/rennudhillon/

CHOOSE TO BE FEARLESS
BY TIFFANY KIEFER

Get out of your own way and reach the confidence you need to succeed.

Dreamer, that is what I was! I was that person who had all of the *great* ideas and spoke about them with enthusiasm. I poured my heart and soul into those ideas, but that is where it stopped. That is what a dreamer does. Well, I am here to tell you, that when *you decide* to stop being that "dreamer" and start being a "*doer*", your life will change.

Being a military wife was one of the hardest and the most rewarding things I have ever done and continue to do in my life. A week after I met my husband,, he told me he loved me as he drove away to live two states away for two years. I was only twenty years old. I remember my dad telling me one night when he tucked me in, "You know, if you marry this guy, he is going to take you away." I will never forget the pain I felt that night. I felt like my world around me was crumbling, and my future was too. Have you ever felt like that? Long story short, we did long distance for two years, got married, and moved to Las Vegas together. It was there that I started the habit of the hand to mouth disorder, more on that to come.

My husband was in the military. Being in the military meant we had to move and I have reinvented myself *numerous* times, *and* frankly so have my kids, but we have never given up.

But, going on, I have a plethora of ideas that *always* run through my head! Have you ever felt like that? Raise your hand if you have had an idea and wanted to talk about it, but didn't for fear of anything? Well, I didn't have that fear. I just blurted it out. I talked, and talked, and talked. *But no action*. That is, again, what a dreamer does. They are *all talk but no action*. Frankly, I was sick of being that person—or rather, "that mom." I wanted to be a mom that my kids would be proud of, one that brought their dreams into reality.

Here is a partial list to give you an idea of the roles I have taken on and/or created over the years. Let's see, not necessarily in this order, but I was a manicurist at one point. I had over fifty clients coming to my home-based business and some of them are still my dearest friends today. I have been top in sales in the timeshare industry, networking marketing, and pleasure sales, earning numerous awards and trips. I even owned my own successful direct sales company, cleaning company for a combined total of fifteen years, and developmental daycare. I also started an apparel and sticker company to make inspirational stickers and sayings. Even with all these accomplished journeys, I never felt fulfilled because I didn't feel that I was helping people. I didn't feel that I was "paying it forward." So, I stand before you today, telling you to reach for the stars. *Reach* for what you want, and what you want will come to you. Please stop consuming yourself with doubt, with food, with addictive bad habits.

That is what I did, with my "hand to mouth disorder" I spoke about earlier. I was so sad and depressed about leaving home, not knowing anyone, not being able to find a good job, that I began to eat and eat—all the way to 312 pounds. That was twenty years ago and I will tell you it has been a *long* journey, but I have been where you are, ready to make a change, ready to stand up and be held accountable, ready to believe in myself.

I am now able to stand before you and share my story and help you become the person that you have always wanted to be because I took that first step. I believed I could. You see, my mother-in-law gave me this bracelet for Christmas this year., it had a saying on it that says: "She believed she could and she did." When she gave that to me, it was a real eye-opener, because I knew she believed in me. Without my mother-in-law really knowing it, she stated that she believed in me and what my journey was about. Now don't get me wrong; my husband and my parents believe in me too, but this was a tangible item, one that I can wear to remind me of the difference that I can make in the world, right here, *right now, with you*! And you can make a difference too! But it requires action, not just words and dreams. We must be willing to take action.

I am going to be totally open and honest with all of you. Today if you met me you might see a person who is a force to be reckoned with,but I will tell you this: Each time we moved from base to base, I became this shy, scared, timid, afraid person who feared, at times, to even go outside. When we moved to England it was cold, dark and scary. I hated it, I hated myself, I hated being there, but I decided that I had to pull up my big girl panties and get over it. I started to exercise daily, even in the blustery cold, I learned to drive on the wrong side of the road on the wrong side of the car (you see, we had brought over our American car), I even learned to volunteer at the elementary school again, which I was petrified. But the true reason I am telling you this is because I did it; I did these things. I went out of my comfort zone and tried. I knew that I may have my side mirror ripped off if I drove too close to the middle of the road, or the kids at the school wouldn't like the games I chose for the afterschool program I started, but I was okay with that, because I was trying.

I even tried to go out for the base softball team. Talk about being petrified. Holy cow. But I made the team, by the skin of my teeth. At forty-one years old, I made the military base softball team! That was a boost to my ego. But what will the team think? What will the younger girls think of me? You see you never know when something is going to help you to help yourself. Help you grow your confidence in yourself. When we moved back to the states, I was afraid to go to the ball field to watch my son play baseball, which is one of the most joyous things I love to do. I was afraid of what they would think of me. I was afraid to go into the gym where my daughter played her sports because I was afraid of what the parents would think of me, a very boisterous loud mom, cheering for her kid. Now I was in civilian land and away from my military family which was way out of my comfort zone.

I felt alone, afraid, scared, judged, singled out, and a little crazy. I am sure some of you reading can relate. I had to learn that none of the opinions of the parents mattered. What truly mattered was how I felt cheering for my child, and how I knew it helped them and the team. What mattered is *how I felt*! We forget that truth.

Here are the key steps of how I overcame my fears and I became the change I wanted to see in the world by starting to look in the mirror at myself.

1. ***Be grateful***. Each day, keep a record of you what happened that day that you are grateful for. I make a point to write down at least ten things. They can be simple things, like the person at the grocery store let me go in front because I only had a few items and they had a cart full. Or it can be a *big* thing like I am grateful my refund check came in the mail.
2. ***Write down your fears and emotions***. Keep a journal about how you are feeling about your fears or situations that happen throughout the day. This will enable you to embrace them, acknowledge them, and start the process of letting go of unhealthy ones. By writing your fears down you are bringing them to the surface, allowing yourself to see them, giving them less power. Writing brings thoughts, fears, and emotions out of your mind and onto paper where you can start to process them, figure out if they really have reason to be a fear or if they are a ridiculous thought. It also helps you acknowledge deep fears that are subconscious. You can begin to process them, and let them go as well.
3. ***Pay attention to your emotions***. How are you feeling? Mastering your emotions is an extremely useful skill. Once you begin to acknowledge how you are feeling in any given situation you can begin to change your thought process and enable yourself to start to feel better.
4. **Meditate daily**. Meditation is proven to help with heart health, increasing your immune system, helping to reduce anxiety, providing more restful sleep, and countless other benefits. Learning to meditate doesn't have to be a challenge. You don't have to sit in the traditional criss cross applesauce regime. You can actually meditate on a nature walk, you can meditate listening to music, you can even laugh as a form of meditation. Some choose to create energy and bonds with meditation like through sex or tantra. All forms are okay, it is what you feel comfortable with and what allows you to go into that deep state of relaxation that allows you to tap into your higher self and power.
5. **Start small.** Fears come in many different shapes and sizes. Not every fear that you face will be important, however, even the smallest of your

fears can break you into a thousand pieces. To be able to fight for your bigger goals, it is important to take smaller steps and keep moving forward. Starting small can help you to reduce your fear and it forces you to take action rather than running from your fears.

6. ***Stop dwelling on scarcity.*** People who tend to quit when things get tough are usually dwelling on scarcity. They accept what little they have and avoid trying harder to accomplish what they want in life. Yes, it is important to be happy with what you have; it is not healthy to dwell on what you don't have. Facing your fears is never an easy process, but it is necessary if you want to become a happier, more productive, person.
7. ***Think positively.*** It is a well-known fact that when you nurture positive thoughts in every aspect of your life, you are better able to attract success, abundance, and prosperity. This is what is known as the law of attraction. To keep fear at bay, you have to make your positive thoughts dominate the negative ones. You can do this by reciting and feeling into daily positive affirmations, focusing on what you want rather than on what you don't want, and drawing into your attention things that help you feel good, rather than things that irritate you or put you in a bad mood. For instance: the news, negative posts on social media, someone else's drama, scary or dangerous movies.

I hope these steps help you choose to release what no longer serves. Use these tips in your daily life, and you'll quickly find that you are able to face all your fears and achieve the success you desire and deserve. Release your fears and step forward powerfully and confidently. If you want to learn more, then please see my contact information listed below. I would love to hear from you and to cheer you on!

Tiffany Kiefer

Hi, my name is Tiffany Kiefer and I believe in creating happiness and love in all areas of my life. I am a retired military wife, a mom of two adult college children, who bring happiness and light to my life every minute of every day.

All of us have busy, filled lives, some with family obligations, not to mention working full-time. Wouldn't it be great if there was a way to enjoy all that you have created?

Just in case you're curious, none of what I have created came by accident and I believe the same or more is possible for you, regardless of your current situation. I have lived through being a victim of sexual molestation as a child, eating disorders, food addictions, being 175 pounds overweight, moving clear across the world to a place I didn't know anyone except my family, and having to start over numerous times in my life. I tried everything I could to stuff my feelings of not being good enough far down into the depths of my soul, but nothing worked. I continuously felt that everyone else was the reason I was so unhappy. I kept thinking that the more things I tried to be successful at, the more I would be liked. Nothing worked, I was constantly in this upward struggle.

So how did I get from there to where I am today, and how does this apply to you? I learned that through self-love you can do anything you put your mind to. I have also learned that the world is made up of energy and you can use this energy to manifest your desires. I know my purpose is to bring hope, healing, and happiness to the world.

Email Address: Riseupnshine777@gmail.com
Phone Number: 408-839-9842
Website Facebook pages: Tiffany Kiefer https://www.facebook.com/groups/Riseupnshine/
LinkedIn page: https://www.linkedin.com/in/tiffany-kiefer-43382139/
Twitter handle: https://twitter.com/epiphanytifany
Instagram: https://www.instagram.com/riseupnshine777/
YouTube Channel: Tiffany Kiefer

SECTION 4:

Step Into Your Power

THE ONLY THING THAT MATTERS IS WHAT YOU BELIEVE!

BY SEEMA GIRI, PMP

I **am on a mission to create a revolution to break free from the expectations, the hold, the power that we allow others to have on us.** I see among so many people, especially women, that it is beginning to tighten the grip so much that it's suffocating them to the point that they are forgetting who they are at the core. Even to the point that they are afraid to be their authentic self. I hope through my journey you will gain some insight, inspiration, and empowerment to find yourself to be able to get back to your authentic self and *be unstoppable*.

I talked about this in my book, *The Authorities*; there's a quiet but pervasive problem in the world today. It's a sense of shame resulting from mental and physical health conditions. People feel they can't speak out, that others won't understand, or it may be even due to shame and being ostracized—and they're right! This is impacting families; it's impacting men, women, and children (who are going to be the leaders of tomorrow). The problem can also be seen as a race to keep up with the acceptable norms of social and economic standards or as we say, "keeping up with the Jones'." Technology has helped increase anxiety with the ease of reach and exposure at the click of a button. You can't get away from the pressures and people's comments.

A critical first step is building a practice of **forgiveness**. How many times before today have you tried to improve your health, improve some aspect of your life, and failed? How many times did you restart a program or recommitted to yourself, "This time I will definitely lose the weight, stop eating junk or exercise daily"? Only to once again not keep up with it How did you react every time you had a setback? If you are anything like me you would have called yourself all kinds of colorful names, including: "you are such a failure", "you are a loser", "you are not good enough", " you are not worthy", or, "so and so was right; you will never amount to anything."

Telling yourself these things doesn't stop at you saying this to yourself once and you are done with it. It plays like a tape recorder without a stop button. It continues on and on every second of every day, damaging each cell in your body. I believe that this was one of the major contributors to my autoimmune disease. I have learned from my experience that if you get illnesses like autoimmune diseases, it's because there are layers of pain, layers of suppressed and unprocessed emotions—you know, the ones you say are okay but that still bother you in your subconscious or like the bottom-most layer of a pile of clothes where you don't see it all the time but you know exactly where it is. It is imperative that you start with forgiving yourself for not being perfect, for not being kind to yourself, for not being loving to yourself. It starts with you, my dear! Start with a clean slate; forgiveness gives you that space to come clean, reset, and restart. Forgiveness of yourself and others is a critical step to help you break free.

Forgive yourself. The supreme act of forgiveness is when you can forgive yourself for all the wounds you've created in your own life. Forgiveness is an act of self-love. When you forgive yourself, self-acceptance begins and self-love grows.

-Miguel Angel Ruiz

Another step to propel yourself forward is to build your confidence through self-esteem and self-love. When you have confidence in yourself and know that taking care of yourself is the most selfless and sacred practice you can do, you will easily be able to take the necessary steps to maintain the consistency that you need to make a deeper and long-lasting impact for yourself.

To reclaim my health, I had to remove each piece of emotion that was buried in that pile. Pick it up, identify it, explore the root cause, hold it, caress it, and love it. At times, it was excruciatingly painful. It was as if I was reliving every moment of that awful experience. I had to process each event, each hurt, and *let it go*. This was the only way I could move forward. I learnt that you can't avoid the painful emotional experience. When you don't deal with your tragedies or heartbreak at the time it happens, it slowly eats away at you; you can delay the inevitable but you can't avoid the pain. By pushing it off to a distant corner where you can still see these painful events from the corner of your eye, you lose focus; you can't concentrate on anything. It takes double or triple the effort to do anything. **It is better that you *stop*. *Pause*. *Breathe* and take *control* of your life *now* and end the pain. Allow yourself to experience the happiness that you deserve.**

While you may never return to the type of life you had or the life as you knew it, **you absolutely have the opportunity to create the life that you want to have *now*.** You have developed into a magnificent person and gained amazing insight and wisdom from your life experiences. **You get to *choose* the impact that you would like to make in this world.** You may even have found your life's purpose which could very well be entirely different from what you had thought of growing up, from what you studied in college or even what your parents or loved ones had expected from you or for you. You know what, your life may even be better than what you had.

Growing up, I always had to ask for permission, even in college up to the point of getting married. Through my healing journey I kept coming to a standstill every time I needed to go to the next level. I finally realized that I was looking for permission, I was looking for another authority to allow me to go to the next level. I realized that we all depend so much on external validation that we don't even check in with ourselves or within us to see what is right for us. **If you are looking for permission, if it is difficult for you to give yourself permission. Right here and right now I give you permission to let go of hurtful experiences and a painful past.** This comes from acknowledging your situation rather than living in denial; take responsibility and make the change. Isn't it time for you to step out of your fear and step into shining your brilliance?

"You can't go back and change the beginning, but you can start where you are and change the ending."
C.S. Lewis

Here is some of my story.

On February 14, 1998, the day of love, I decided it was time to shine my brilliance. I made the **decision**, no matter what, I will do everything in my power to heal. The experts are right. You have to have a big audacious why to be able to make the transformation. Mine was providing a beautiful life for my son. Being part of his life, I wanted my baby to know who I am and how much I loved him.

What is your big audacious why? It would be wonderful if your why is you. It's okay if it is not for yourself yet. The important thing is that you get started like I did. As you work through this, I promise you that in time your big audacious why will be *you*!

That day, I realized three things:

- **My life is in my control**
- **I always have choices**
- **The only thing that really matters is what I believe**

I started dreaming big. I imagined all the activities I do with my son. How I would take him to the park, teach him to walk. All the activities from nursery school, elementary school, to college, to his wedding, and even grandchildren. I imagined our family celebrating special moments together and traveling the world.

That day I felt like Superwoman and I was standing like one lying down. I didn't know the how, but I knew, no matter what, I was going to heal.

I began to be courageously unstoppable. I didn't know what to do, or how to do it. I was scared but I took *action* anyway.

Have you ever had a moment where life brought you to your knees so that you would be forced to make a decision that would forever change your life?

This was my wake-up call. The universe sends you signs and messages if you don't understand or understand and don't take action. It will whack you upside your head until you pay attention. Boy, was I paying attention now! I discovered I was not playing full out in my life. I was playing small and hiding behind the excuses called the Indian culture, strict upbringing, being a girl, and not having choices.

What area of your life are you playing small and what excuse are you hiding behind?

What do your excuses look like? Do any of these resonate?

- I am so busy
- There are so many things going on at home and at work
- Too many people depend on me
- I don't have enough time
- I don't have enough money
- I don't have family
- I don't have friends
- I don't have the skills
- I don't have the courage
- I don't know how
- I am not qualified

This is an endless list. What areas of your life you are playing small? I suggest getting a piece of paper and a pen, and write it down as the first thoughts come to your mind.

Because I had lost so much precious time, I hired several coaches to achieve my goals faster—the best investment I ever made in myself. Through their tested systems, life experiences, and the perfect balance of empathy, the ability to show me my blind spots, and not allowing me to hide, I got unbelievable results quickly. As I continued my journey, working with various therapists, counselors, and coaches, I realized how many suppressed and unprocessed emotions I had bottled up inside. These were tough and scary to get through. It took several years of processing and removing layer after layer of emotion, but I managed to get closer to the core of the onion. There were some key pivotal moments that really impacted my life, but I kept peeling away those layers, one at a time. **While it may take some time to peel all of the layers one at a time, in the meantime, I am living my best life ever.** I have had major breakthroughs that have given me the blessings to help women like you have wonderful gifts to share in the world, who deserve more. Women have been empowered to come out of the shadows, have quantum leaps in their mindset, and become unstoppable in business and life through programs I have been able to bring forward to support them.

If you have to settle for things in life, then why not settle for more? Remember, you have full permission to step forward in those areas that matter most to you.

You have so much potential in you; you have a wonderful gift within you that you are here to share in this world. There are people waiting for someone exactly like you!

"You don't become what you want, you become what you believe."
Oprah Winfrey

Be Unstoppable Steps

1. Forgive yourself and others
2. Build your confidence and self-love
3. Get support from family, friends, and professionals
4. Honor the journey and choose to be unstoppable
5. It is okay to be afraid, to feel fear, but take action anyway
6. Give yourself permission
7. Choose to live your best life *now*!

Seema Giri

As a holistic lifestyle strategist and an expert on bouncing back from adversity, Seema teaches busy women how they can rebound, reset, and realign themselves whenever they are faced with adversity. Through the use of her proprietary system, professional women are empowered to come out of the shadows, have quantum leaps in their mindset, and become unstoppable in business and life.

Seema Giri is an award-winning author, international speaker, and coach. She has spoken across the US to various audiences and her professional experience spans over twenty years in project management, having trained and coached over 100,000 individuals. Seema is the co-author of the book *The Authorities* co-authored with *New York Times* bestselling author Dr. John Gray, from the Mars/Venus series in which she shares her transformational story of suffering from being bedridden with chronic pain to becoming a successful entrepreneur and showing others how to do the same through the use of her proprietary system.

FB: https://www.facebook.com/seemagiri.standinyourpower/
Twitter: https://twitter.com/giriseema
Instagram: https://www.instagram.com/giriseema1
FB group:
https://www.facebook.com/groups/breakfreetostandinyourpower/
LinkedIn: www.linkedin.com/in/seema-giri-embracebrilliance

THE SMARTER WAY TO PROMOTE YOURSELF

BY JŌS HANAN

Have you ever felt frustrated about promoting something? Maybe you were promoting your business, your child's fundraiser, or your favorite cause.

My Quest Started with Cookie Sales

I started questioning how to be a smarter promoter when I was a kid, selling Girl Scout cookies in the Chicago cold.

I loved Girl Scouts, going on camping trips, and being a top cookie seller for ten years. However, I did not love ringing doorbells when my fingers were so cold I could no longer feel them. It was especially annoying when families heard the doorbell and then hurried to turn off their lights, as if they weren't home. That's doubly cold!

I kept thinking there had to be a better way to make money and make a difference.

But how can we work smarter promoting what we believe in? This became my lifelong power question.

Where There's Water, There's Answers

Sometime around junior year of high school I had my first answer.

Our family had just flown from Chicago to Florida, and Dad was driving our rental car on the expressway to our hotel. When he saw a billboard that said, "Wet 'N' Wild Ahead," Dad said: "Girls, if you have your swimsuits, I'm taking you here."

I was so excited. First, I love waterparks. And second, I thought like an entrepreneur (and didn't even know it).

I kept thinking to myself: "Wet 'N' Wild did not approach us: They did not call us or knock on our door. Dad saw a billboard, and he decided to go to them!"

I also saw a huge line of families who were paying admission too.

Accordingly, I asked Dad, "What's it called when you put up a sign and then people buy what you're selling?"

Dad responded, "That's called advertising."

My decision to earn an advertising degree became a no-brainer.

From Promoting Girl Scouts to Promoting Women Entrepreneurs

In addition to earning an advertising degree, I also earned a "minor" in women's studies, which is the most "major" degree I've ever received!

After accumulating over a decade of experience in the marketing world (and a lifetime of experience putting on events for women and girls), I founded Promote Her Business (PHB) International. PHB is "a hybrid between a *virtual networking* group and a year-round *marketing and sales training* program." I am passionate about teaching women entrepreneurs to "work smarter" by learning the best ways to promote themselves and each other, while building win-win profitable relationships both locally and globally.

For the rest of this article, I'm excited to share best practices in promotion with you. Practices which our global PHB community leverages throughout the year and practices I wish I would have known when I was a Girl Scout.

What to Do When You're Desperate

You know what breaks my heart? It's when people have great products, services, and fundraisers, and they're giving it their all, but they're not getting results!

Many people don't know how to bridge the gap between wanting to serve more people and figuring out how to do it fast enough. This often causes them to feel desperate, and there's nothing wrong with that! *Feeling desperate is a healthy sign that you're aligned with what you're passionate about, and you care so much, it hurts.*

In Girl Scouts, there were many years that I felt desperate to hit my goals, especially when I was less than 100 boxes away and had less than a month to sell them.

The issue isn't that you're feeling desperate, the issue is how you react to that feeling.

On the one hand, desperation can cause people to act in a way that *often turns off the very audience they're hoping to attract.*

For example: People will put flyers on windshields, hard sell their audience during talks, spam friends on social media, and turn networking into one-sided sales pitches.

Sadly, it's not even a debate on if "the means justify the ends" because there are *no ends*. They're not producing results; they're just producing a damaged reputation! Their choice to use desperate techniques are causing them to be avoided, left off their friends/family invitation lists, and kicked out of networking groups.

Can you admit to yourself "desperate" promotion techniques you've used?

On the other hand, desperation can also cause people to feel powerless and avoid selling. Sometimes people are so desperate to be liked that they're afraid to be perceived like a "salesperson" even when everyone knows they're selling something. They'll say: "I only focus on sharing, not selling." Oftentimes, *they get what they focus on*, and they're sharing with a lot of people but not selling to them.

I was able to sell over 500 boxes of Girl Scout cookies for years, because my Girl Scout leader, who was my mom, taught me to have a specific sales target. I knew that selling 300 versus 500 boxes would directly affect both my prize and our troop's camping trips. Accordingly, when I was feeling cold or tired, knowing that I still had *x* more cookie boxes to sell motivated me to keep ringing doorbells in a way that just sharing until I ran out of energy wouldn't have.

So, what should you do when you're feeling desperate?

1. **Admit it,** as opposed to pretending you're above feeling desperate. Acknowledge yourself for caring so much. Being in tune with feeling desperate will help you avoid being blindsided by your reaction to it.
2. **Seek support:** Promoting yourself can be very challenging. *There's a big difference between being great at what you do versus being great at promoting what you do!*
3. **Expand your options:** Feeling desperate may also indicate that you're feeling like you're out of options, so learn more choices for promoting yourself.

There's No Shame in Asking for Support

Marketing is constantly changing, and everyone can stand to get better at sales, as it's the life blood of any business. Accordingly, there is zero shame in feeling confused or like you need to hire support. That's expected!

Most people were never formally taught marketing and/or sales. Were you?

Even if you are a marketing/sales expert, wouldn't you agree it's still hard to keep up? You could have a full-time job just trying to understand Facebook, let alone all the other ways to promote yourself.

With that said, if you interview an "expert," who claims they can help you with "everything" in marketing and sales, do *not* hire them. *Run away from them faster than a Girl scout runs away from people who "already bought last year."*

No expert knows "everything." The best experts are continually learning, and they know when to refer you to people outside of their skill set.

Smarter Ways to Promote What Matters

Overall, what's the best advice this Girl Scout-at-heart can give you to work smarter and have more fun as you're doing it?

1. **Think Outside the (Cookie) Box**: Just because a promotion strategy works for someone else doesn't mean it will work for you. My Girl Scout leader, my mom, was my sales role model. However, the way she sold cookies—by telling funny, heartwarming stories about her daughters—didn't work for me. I had to find my own words to sell. Even if you're working off a "duplicatable" script, it's still important to make it sound authentically you. I'm not my mom, and you're not your upline, your sales coach, or the best promoter you know. Make the script your own because people don't buy cookies. *They buy cookies, because they're from* you!
   <u>Promotion Tip:</u> Be more you. *How can you incorporate more of your personality into your script and have it sound more authentically you?*

2. **Explore doing "Business Her Way" (no matter your gender):** For most of history, the masculine—a strong, competitive, and results-driven

energy—has been regarded as "the energy" to step into for business results. Although the masculine has advantages, consider stepping into your feminine power more, because it can help you become more attractive to your ideal audience. Now-a-days the world of marketing/ sales is very "feminized": It's a world of "sharing", "loving", being socially conscious, paying it forward, and playing to emotions (since people buy on emotion and justify with logic). Playing to the feminine may also help you resonate more with the 70–80 percent of women that make all the consumer purchasing decisions!
Promotion Tip: Create an emotional advantage. *Review one piece of written marketing material. How can you add more emotion, stories, and feeling to it?*

3. **Collaborate more:** If I could have improved something about Girl Scouts, I would have suggested that Girl Scout troops share best practices at the end of each cookie season. Collaboration could also mean joining forces on bigger marketing efforts, which could benefit everyone. Our troop couldn't have afforded a billboard, but if we united our funding across troops, it could have been different. Who knows? Families could have lined up for cookies like they did for Wet 'N' Wild waterslides.
   Promotion Tip: Think in terms of "we." Instead of thinking about how you can persuade your ideal audience to buy something, act as if "we are in this together." *How does collaborative energy—as opposed to competitive "I'm going to sell you" energy—affect what you say and how you act toward them?*

4. **Make Tech Your Friend:** As Girl Scouts sing: "Make new friends, but keep the old;" it is especially important to make "new friends" with technology if you have avoided it! Technology is no longer "nice to have"; *technology is a must-have to "work smarter" when promoting anything.* Virtual technology helps you get in front of more people faster, saves you time, and has capabilities you don't have in-person. For example: In our Promote Her Business community, although we have local networking circles, we're also big fans of doing Virtual Networking via video conference. Women entrepreneurs love networking from the comfort of their computer. Let's say a mom-preneur is asking other women to buy her daughter's Girl Scout cookies: She can share her screen to show camping trips, a picture of her daughter's badges, and even the ingredients on the back of the cookie box.

Promotion Tip: Be "virtually" smarter. *How else can you promote yourself online?* How can you network with more of your ideal audience virtually? Are you using the visual nature of the online world to your advantage? Think pictures, videos, and not just saying it, but showing it.

5. **Never Let Someone Take Away Your Badge of Honor:** Earning my Girl Scout Gold Award, the highest award in Girl Scouts, was one of the proudest moments of my life. However, when I was a college freshman, I let my advisor take my pride away. My advisor told me to take my Gold Award off my resume, because "employers won't take you seriously." My eyes flooded with tears, as I was wrongly led to believe that companies would think my thirteen years of Girl Scout accomplishments—and hard-earned badges of honor—were a "joke"! It took me years, but I finally came to realize that I should never put someone else's opinion above my own truth. And my truth is that my Girl Scout Gold Award is such a *big deal* that I'm still proudly telling the world about it today, at age thirty-eight!
   Promotion Tip: Honor your truth. Who has said something negative about what you're promoting? *Revisit what is true for you. Honor yourself for standing up for who you are and what you promote*
   Here's to promoting what matters to you: Online. Offline. All the Time.

Jōs Hanan

Jōs Hanan is the CEO/Founder of Promote Her Business (PHB) International, which is a "hybrid between a *virtual networking* group and year-round *marketing and sales training* program" for supportive and purpose-driven women entrepreneurs across industries and experience levels. Jōs is a strategic messaging coach and speaker who supports women entrepreneurs across industries to "write in a way that sells and compels."

Jōs has expertise in copywriting, training design/development, marketing strategy, sales training, event facilitation, leadership development, advanced networking, public speaking, and women and entrepreneurship.

For over a decade, Jōs has specialized in working with businesses across industries to UPlevel their marketing and communications; develop strong leaders; and design, develop, and facilitate business training. Jōs has worked in corporate, nonprofit, and academic settings, as well as had the government as a client. She has consulted with Fortune 500s and has had small businesses of her own, so she can directly relate to the pains and passions of entrepreneurs! Jōs' biggest passion is helping more women entrepreneurs discover their "signature message" and have it be remembered, repeated, and responded to!

Jos@PromoteHerBusiness.com
(408) 916-5742
www.PromoteHerBusiness.com
Friends of Promote Her Business (Public Facebook group):
https://www.facebook.com/groups/494087833965041/
Promote Her Business (Facebook Business Page):
https://www.facebook.com/PromoteHerBusiness/?ref=br_rs
LinkedIn (Personal Profile):
https://www.linkedin.com/in/josephinehanan713/
Promote Her Business (LinkedIn group):
https://www.linkedin.com/groups/4868736/
Twitter: @PromoteHerBiz
Silicon Valley Networking Circle on Meetup:
www.Meetup.com/Promote-Her-Business

BREAKING FREE WITH MINDFULNESS
BY MICHELLE SUGIYAMA

Have you ever held a secret so shameful or humiliating that you kept it from your parents, your husband, and even your best friends? You've hidden it for such a long time that it was almost forgotten. Now and again, it gives you a tug and you yearn to be free from the self-induced prison.

For over thirty years, I stored this type of secret. If unleashed, it would expose my flaw, my defect; and I would be left raw and open for judgment, ridicule, and possibly abandonment. Although I wanted to release this albatross, I never had the strength or wherewithal to disclose it to anyone.

Well, you know the old saying, "everything happens for a reason." All your actions, experiences, and social connections lead you to something. With one conversation, this happened to me. I was invited to speak about mindful eating and health at an empowerment conference in Las Vegas. After much deliberation, I decided it was finally time, but more importantly, help empower 400 women. And, why not, because what happens in Vegas, stays in Vegas!

I was honored, nervous, and excited all at the same time. For many people, mindful eating can be a new and perplexing topic but also relevant in today's society. With the luxuries of the 21st century, many of us are very disconnected with our food and our relationship with it. We can buy exotic food that's been shipped for thousands of miles. With smartphones and a few clicks, our meals can be delivered right to our door. And oftentimes we mindlessly wolf down food without appreciating its beauty, flavors, and how it can heal us.

From personal experience, I can tell you what mindful eating is not. It is not standing at your kitchen pantry shoving in whatever you can find, devouring a large buttered popcorn at the movies till you feel sick, or gorging on a huge piece of chocolate cake while crying your eyes out. Drowning out anxiety, stress, or depression plus hating yourself for being disgusting and weak.

On stage at the conference, I confessed that I have done all those things and more. My heart raced as I finally declared, "For fifteen years, I suffered from an eating disorder." With one short phrase, a huge weight was lifted and I was relieved that there were no judgmental stares or whispers. As a matter of fact, I received a lot of compliments and was elated that I could uplift so many lives.

Even if an eating disorder has never touched your world, please keep reading. You'll come away with insights and easy, practical tools to supercharge your energy, focus, immunity, inflammation, metabolism, overall health, and even happiness. Your health can most certainly affect your happiness and science is showing that happiness can affect your health.[3]

As a health coach, chef, and speaker, my gift is to positively impact people's lives with partnership and sound science. Over the years, I've seen some wonderful changes. Take Jessie, a busy super mom, who always felt bloated and unhappy with her body. After working together, she has more energy, is less bloated, and loves her newfound confidence.

I'd like to share my story in the hopes that it will help you break free to stand in your power.

---

3. https://www.healthline.com/nutrition/happiness-and-health

While my disorder started in high school, I felt like an outsider since kindergarten, desperate to fit in. During the 1970s, racism was alive and well in the Carolinas. I was teased, called a chink, and mocked by kids slanting their eyes with their pointer fingers. Although I wanted to cower and hide, I would just stand there like a deer in headlights. As you can imagine, I did not want to be oriental (PC at the time), eat white rice, and use chopsticks. I wanted fried chicken, creamy mashed potatoes, and green beans from a can. Fortunately, my family moved to the north and, while still a minority, I felt accepted and gained some good friendships.

The transition to high school had a rocky start. Luckily, I was fairly coordinated and with tons of practice, I made the cheerleading squad. I was thrilled that I might finally fit in! My celebration was cut short when a few girls asked me to quit. If I bowed out, their friend, the alternate, would make the team. I was absolutely crushed but there was no way in hell they were going to win. I did not cower; I did not quit. Even if I was going to be the black sheep, I was going to stay in control. And just like that, my eating disorder began.

When it would rear its ugly head, I would say to myself, "Oh, you can stop at any time," or "It will never happen again." Twelve years later, with many relapses, I found myself in corporate America working an unfulfilling job, constantly on the road, stressed, and in an unhappy marriage. I had no idea that, in my late twenties, I was having anxiety attacks. I could never really explain my symptoms other than I felt like I was going to die. Depression set in and I felt like I had lost complete control of my life, suffering from a culmination of so many things and trying to gain control the only way I knew how.

Unfortunately, I never considered psychotherapy, probably due to social stigma or having to admit I had a problem. But, I knew one thing: this eating disorder was going to kill me. Thankfully, I pulled myself out of the muck and am astounded by the current statistics: At least 30 million people of all ages and genders suffer from an eating disorder in the US. Every sixty-two minutes at least one person dies as a direct result from an eating disorder. Eating disorders have the highest mortality rate of any mental illness and 13 percent of women over fifty engage in eating disorder behaviors.[4] I also learned that you don't need to be bulimic or anorexic to have an eating disorder. Tell-tale signs, due to food or body image, are depression, anxiety and general unhappiness, or spending a large percentage of time thinking about them which interferes with everyday life.

As I thought about how I beat the odds, a handful of things stuck out: Believing in my own truths, being kind to myself, and incorporating mindfulness into a healthy lifestyle. I'd like to expand on mindfulness and health since I wish I would have known then, what I know now.

Mindfulness is about being aware. Living fully present in the moment without dwelling in the past or hoping for the future. Mindful eating is about slowing down to notice your state of body, mind, and environment. Plus, taking time to enjoy the smells, colors, textures, and tastes of your food without criticism or self-judgment.

Putting mindful eating into practice is key. If this is a new concept for you, start with baby steps. For example, recognize what triggers you to grab food when you're not truly hungry. Is it from an external cause, like *seeing* that perfectly baked apple pie or *smelling* the mouthwatering scent of chocolate chip cookies? Could it be from an emotion, say anger, that causes you to grab a bag of potato chips? Emotions can be powerful triggers, which I'll definitely discuss later.

For years, I've taught a chocolate and mindfulness workshop at many corporations and other venues. Participants learn about, appreciate, smell, savor, and identify flavors in different brands of chocolate. It's always been well received and many are amazed at their reactions. One woman realized that she didn't even like the brand of chocolate she's been bingeing on for years! It now tasted gritty, artificial, and mass-produced. Another was surprised that, with such a small amount, her sweet tooth was completely satisfied. Since it takes about twenty minutes for your brain and stomach to connect, simply slowing down can prevent you from overeating.

Take a moment and think about why you eat when you're not truly hungry. There are about six reasons. I know you'll want to get to all the

---

4. https://anad.org/education-and-awareness/about-eating-disorders/eating-disorders-statistics/

chapters in this book so I'll expand on three and give you simple tools to avoid them.

1. Thirst can be a trickster. We think we're hungry when we're actually thirsty. If this might be the case, drink a nice tall glass of water and decide if you still need to eat.

Hydrating is also a great way to start the day. You're most likely dehydrated which can cause fatigue, mood swings, brain fog, and headaches. Place a large glass of water on your nightstand so it's the first thing you see in the morning. Before heading for the coffee maker, guzzle that right down. If you can't fathom the thought, start with a small amount of water and work your way up.

You may be wondering, "How much water should I drink per day?" It can depend on your body weight, activity level, and climate you live in. You are the expert of your body, but a good rule of thumb is to drink half your weight in fluid ounces. If you weigh 160 pounds, you'll want to strive for eighty ounces of pure water, but other non-caffeinated drinks and water-rich foods can add to your fluid balance. Find a water bottle you love to carry around, preferably stainless steel. Determine its volume in ounces so you know how many bottles to drink.

2. Emotional states, especially negative emotions, are biggies. We overindulge on (unhealthy) comfort food to numb our anger, stress, sadness, disappointment, frustration, anxiety, and so much more.

I obviously binge ate when I was stressed or depressed but also when I was frustrated. Back in the day, computers would crash incessantly. When I wanted to toss my computer out the window, I would grab something crunchy. And, if it was crunchy and salty, that was twice as nice. I would mindlessly munch away in front of the computer, the source of my frustration! Then, I would get upset for eating way too much. What I should have done was acknowledge my frustration and allow one serving to truly comfort me. Or pick a healthier option like going for a quick walk, listening to music, taking deep belly breaths, or meditating.

3. The gut microbiome is a hot topic in health and wellness. Remarkably, our body contains far more bacterial cells than human cells! Scientists are finding that the microbiome is connected to many things

like brain function, cravings, digestion, immunity, weight, and chronic disease. It can be problematic when our microbiome is out of balance —? in other words, the bad bacteria outnumber the good.

The great news is that you can quickly make positive changes to your microbiome, even just after 24 hours. By flooding your body with clean fruits and vegetables, you can start to balance your microbiome plus naturally detox without starvation. The fiber, antioxidants, and thousands of other plant chemicals work together to keep us healthy at a cellular level. By balancing the microbiome along with a healthy lifestyle, my clients have experienced astonishing results. For example, Andrea's plaque psoriasis, an autoimmune disease that hit her at age fourteen, drastically improved by 90 percent. After twenty-five years of Irritable Bowel Syndrome (IBS) and severe bloating, Steve's symptoms came to a halt!

While this is just a tip of the nutritional iceberg, I hope you'll try to incorporate some these healthy lifestyle tools:

- Practice mindful eating to become aware of your body, mind, and environment; and enjoy your food without criticism or self-judgment.
- Hydrate right away and throughout the day. With pure water, strive for half your body weight in fluid ounces.
- Notice emotional states. If you're not truly hungry, choose a healthy option like going for a walk or deep breathing.
- Balance your microbiome. Aim for ten handfuls of fruits and vegetables every day to feed your good bacteria.

You definitely don't have to try them all at once. Pick one of these tools and start incorporating it right away. After a few weeks, incorporate another and then another. Before long, they'll become lifestyle habits. You'll be on the road to a healthier, happier you so your inner light can truly shine. Start today because your health is truly #1.

Michelle Sugiyama

Michelle Sugiyama, MS, engages, inspires, and empowers people to take control of their health. While she is the founder of Mindful Eating, a Master Certified health coach, nutritional chef and national speaker, Michelle did not begin her career in wellness. She received a Master's in chemistry and then quit corporate America after ten long years. Michelle became a top honors graduate at Le Cordon Bleu Culinary Arts with an externship in Southern France and founded a personal chef company so families could have healthy conversations and food around their own dinner table. She also went back into corporate America as the highlight of numerous employee wellness programs with captivating seminars, culinary demonstrations, and mouthwatering dishes. Michelle's passion for lifelong education and service lead her to a health coaching certification and is on track to become Board Certified in late 2020.

For over fifteen years, Michelle has enhanced the wellness of busy women, children, seniors, and employees at mid-sized to Fortune 100 companies by bridging the gap between knowing you should be healthy and actually doing it. While science-based, with a focus on the microbiome, she gives simple, effective, and practical tools so you can truly enjoy the golden half of life. Michelle's inspirations are her nine-year-old adopted daughter and 101-year-old grandmother whose mantra was *health is #1.*

https://www.facebook.com/michelle.sugiyama
www.mindful-eating.com
https://www.facebook.com/MindfulEatingNow/

THE JOURNEY TO WHOLENESS AS THE SURVIVING TWIN

BY DEBORAH WIENER

Where is my best friend? This question was the focus of my attention most of my life. I lost my identical twin sister in my mother's womb at the end of her second trimester of pregnancy. Even at birth I needed a strong will to survive. I overcame the umbilical cord wrapped around my neck. Losing my twin (although I did not know it for a great majority of my child and adult life), I came to understand was tied into my inability to maintain long-term relationships.

Losing my identical twin sister left me with a sense that something was missing. I couldn't explain the feeling, but it put me in a perpetual search for a special friend. The longing for a strong connection with someone I could trust and count on was deep inside me, but often went unfulfilled. That feeling of being unable to attract a person to be as committed to me as I was to them often left me in pain and despair. I began to realize for much of my life, I based my own happiness or fulfillment on being completed by another person.

I can think of two examples in my youth and in my young adult life that highlight the exact nature of what I am talking about. The first time was in my childhood. I had a longtime friend who I thought was my best friend at the time, right up until she got married, and I was not invited. I could not understand this. In fact, it was years before we spoke again, but I can easily recall the pain of being left out. The second time was when I was an adult and had already moved to California. I went back to visit my family and friends, or at least who I thought were still my friends. I was very disappointed when my longtime friend would not travel two miles to come visit me. I did not have access to a car, so I thought for sure she would come, alas I found out she was not as close to me as I was to her.

I encountered many people along the way who I thought would help complete my search for my missing "best friend," however, this was not the case. Often because I would immediately take to another person much faster than they would take to me, I would end up disappointed or worse, feeling rejected.

The emotional impact of losing my twin compounded with my childhood experiences resulted in a sense of loss, abandonment, loneliness, and disillusionment in my life. Some of those lessons were learned from my siblings. At a young age, I was asked to watch my younger brother and sisters. Often, I was the parent. The burden of trying to be the parent while still being a child myself left me in a constant state of rejection from my parents and my siblings which then caused resentment toward my younger siblings.

As I grew up, I did evolve from some of these patterns, yet these patterns remained between me and one of my sisters. Her independent streak when she was young only worsened matters for me, since she was the closest to me in age as I saw her like being a twin (meaning best friend for life); yet she often left the house without notice, did things for herself, which I then interpreted as selfish and acting out against me. She has a ferociously independent spirit. When younger she refused to be confined and controlled, to "toe the line," so to speak. She exerted her independence to become the free spirit she is.

Growing up in our home was dysfunctional. I did not know my birth father until I was nineteen. My stepfather was not equipped to deal with my mother's death; he was an alcoholic who would verbally abuse me and my older sister. Most times physical abuse seemed moments away and I was terrified to be home alone with him. He forced me to do all the cleaning and cooking while taking care of my three younger siblings.

I continued to look for a best friend I often felt unsafe in my own home, leading to feelings of abandonment and despair. These experiences also caused me to have unhealthy relationships. I constantly sought out relationships where I had a purpose and in my distorted perception that would cause me to believe I would not be alone which meant safety in my mind.

After our mother passed away when I was twelve, the situation with my stepfather and siblings worsened. The next five years only made it more imperative I leave. At seventeen I could no longer stay at home and left for college. However, since I had yet to learn the lessons I needed to learn, I continued the habit of thinking my friends were for life and very close to me while only being disappointed again for this flawed way of thinking.

I have spent most of life seeking advice from others. I have been in therapy with professional counseling, attended seminars about improving oneself, and currently have many spiritual advisors who have helped me learn to be a better person. The road has been long and windy, two steps forward one step back. The process of self-improvement is ongoing. I continue to grow and with the help of others, I hope to always grow.

I realized that there was great value in the lessons learned by the experiences with my sister. It propelled me to learn what is real and what is not real. What can be taken away is not real—that dependency outside yourself on someone else. The only person you can depend on is yourself!

I learned a lot by observing my own twin sons and my identical twin granddaughters. Twins look to each other for their answers, opinions, needs, love, support, connection, and friendship. Even though all the while looking for their own identity and individuality with a feeling that they are not enough. It is a struggle. The lesson is not on dependency, but shared relationships coming from a place of strength, faithfulness, and that allow the freedom to be an individual.

I discovered the lesson is to be in relationships, not in an unhealthy way. I learned to build relationships that are not dependent on each other for completion and wholeness, not from a place of "I need you" to create a codependency due to a shared identity. This type of relationship is destined to implode so that one can find their own identity. Instead, build a relationship coming from a place of wholeness.

I learned that when your perspective comes from wounding, the wounding gives distorted confusing perspectives. When assumptions come from feelings of abandonment, victimization, and wounding, the assumptions lose their objectivity and personalization and distorted beliefs jump in to create false assumptions, false realities, and fear (false experiences appearing real).

This statement rings true for me: You find that which you seek most, when you are not seeking it at all. Dependency causes one to look outside themselves for answers. The gift is the realization that the answers are inside! Looking inside versus outside was a complete validation of my own identity! I can have deep, close, shared connections. My twin lives within me energetically. She is not lost and has not abandoned me. The paradox between those interdependent on each other and the need for individuality and close, deep connections is now clear. I now look within myself rather than outside myself. Resolving these issues by taking responsibility for my actions as opposed to asking others to change theirs has been a very difficult and powerful lesson for me to absorb. I often expected others to change instead of changing myself. I did not know I needed to change, nor that I even had the strength to do so, before I undertook this journey.

Today, I have been happily married for thirty-two years. My husband has been by my side through all my growth and pains, and he has shown me what a best friend is truly about. Often, we would battle and argue, and no matter what, he was always there. When we did argue he would tell me we cannot go to bed mad, and we would end up talking all night long. We have three terrific sons who honor me with unconditional love and warmth, and I easily return those feelings. These boys of ours are why I can truly say I understand what is important about relationships and why they are important. Nothing has been better in my life than being a mother. I now know what it feels like to experience unconditional love. I am truly blessed.

Now that I am coming from this new space there is a room for the use of my own intuition. Dependency got in the way of using my intuition. I now can trust myself as well as my intuition. I can now see in others the pain they have in the same manner that I no longer have. Seeing others suffer is in no way a positive feeling yet knowing that I can see and understand their pain, empathize with it, and not feel it myself, is the truest form of growth.

The completion of unhealthy relationships ultimately ended with the opportunity to discover within myself a desire for deep connections in my relationships. While looking back at some of those relationships and experiences, I can find humor in many of them. I have learned that my future lessons to learn can be lighthearted and gentle versus painful and hard.

I was looking for love in all the wrong places! Love must first be found from within. When you love yourself, when you find that place to love from within, then you can love others. I have been searching for healing my entire life while seeking connection through wisdom and managing my emotions. To be able to do all of that now is truly a gift.

Today I realize stepping into my *own* power could not have happened without doing the following:

1 Admit responsibility for your own actions.
2 Understanding that what others say or do does not define who you are.
3 Forgive yourself and forgive others, especially those close to you.
4 Realize you must look at situations from many points of view, not just yours.
5 Listen to your intuition, trust it, and step into your power.
6 Know that you are enough just as you are.
7 Learn who you are to find your authentic self.
8 Learn to love and celebrate who you are.

Deborah Wiener

Deborah Wiener has a great deal of experience in the world of twins. She lost her identical twin sister in utero. She had fraternal boy/girl twin cousins growing up. She has identical twin nephews. She has fraternal twin boys. She has identical twin granddaughters.

Deborah grew up always looking for her best friend. She always had a feeling of wanting to be closer to her girlfriends. Sometimes she would want to be around her friends longer than they would want to be around her. Maybe her neediness pushed them away. The rejection she felt in not understanding that just because she lost her twin, she still had the same needs a twin has. She was still a twin!

The needs of an identical twin are even greater than those of fraternal twins. Identical twins are best friends for life! They have their own languages only they can understand. They have unconditional love for each other. They are sometimes too close. They never are very far away from each other. They talk to each other all day as children and often as adults.

My twin nephews still lived with each other when the first twin married. He lived in the finished basement until his brother introduced him to his current wife. They live a mile from each other. They both married similar looking wives, and each have three children.

If you are a twin, have twins, know twins, or are curious about their behaviors, I will be writing more information in my upcoming chapter on twins.

https://www.facebook.com/deborah.l.wiener
DWiener@quickscrews.com

REVIEWS

"Break Free to Stand in Your Power is an elegant and inspiring collection of chapters. Reading these magical stories and imbibing the many life lessons shared in them will cause your spirits to soar to greater heights and help you achieve your full potential."

-Dr. Sanjiv Chopra, Professor of Medicine at Harvard Medical School Best Selling Author

"These journeys of transformation and the triumph of the human spirit will enlighten, inspire and motivate you to embrace your own unlimited potential."

-Heather Burgett, award-winning publicist and CEO/founder of The Burgett Group, Inc. and PR Stars Online Programs (prstars.net)

"I found Break Free to Stand in Your Power deeply inspiring. Each chapter is an incredible guide to breaking free from whatever may be holding you back in your life. Themes ranged from don't give up, to changing your mindset, to having a burning desire, to honoring the innate gifts we all have, to changing your diet, to that we are limitless and that we can achieve whatever we set our minds to and that forgiveness is a critical step to break free. People are waiting for your gifts. Give yourself a gift and soak up the profound words in this book."

-Carol Fitzgerald, Author of 6 books, Sr. Model, YouTuber
Health Care Advocate
Website: www.carolfitzgerald.net
IG: carolfitzgerald5
YouTube: www.youtube.com/user/thecarobi5

"In Break Free to Stand in Your Power, Seema Giri has compiled a group of interesting and different authors who bring you into their world. These authors describe in their own words the who, what, why, and where they had their awakening moment. Their experiences and expectations were intriguing and thought-provoking to say the least. I would recommend this book to anyone who is going through a tough time or wanting to change the direction of their life. The thoughtfulness and examples of how they made the changes needed to correct the direction of their life into who they are now are awe-inspiring and will definitely help you to take a different look at what you are going through."

-Elizabeth Clamon, COO, The Clamon Group, International Bestselling Author, Professional Speaker, and Life and Business Coach
https://elizabethclamon.com
https://Facebook.com/ElizabethClamonspeaker/
https://www.linkedin.com/in/elizabeth-clamon-336b5413b/
https://www.youtube.com/channel/UCJSb3Q8Gte7RMTkP7ZflF9g

"Beautiful stories of strong individuals who discovered themselves through their struggles and their challenges in life while finding true meaning, pursuing their dreams, and overcoming that which was holding them back. Diverse, courageous, unique look into the lives of several powerful characters!"

-Elle Ballard
Entrepreneur, World Traveler, Speaker, Founder of WOTWN
www.elleballard.com

"Seema Giri has pulled together an impressive group of authors who share their powerful personal stories and the even more powerful lessons they learned from those experiences. From those lessons, the authors gleaned precious bits of guidance to assist others in moving to their own place of power, acceptance, and brilliance by "breaking free" of those patterns, persons, behaviors—anything at all—that no longer serve the journey. It will be a cherished instrument toward helping many to journey to their rightful place of power!"

-Nancy Tarr Hart, PhD
#1 International Best-Selling Author, Chair and Assistant Professor of Philosophy
tarrheart@gmail.com
www.walkinginwisdom.life
https://www.facebook.com/nancy.t.hart.9
https://www.facebook.com/wisdom's.daughters.community.circles

CLOSING THOUGHTS

Dear Amazing Reader,

I hope you enjoyed and were touched by these powerful chapters. Each author has carefully handpicked stories from challenging times in their lives so they could inspire, educate, and empower you to realize your brilliance, to give you a sense of hope and encouragement, and to let you know you are not alone.

We can't wait for you to break free and stand in your power and to celebrate you as you share your wonderful gifts with the world.

I would like to share additional resources that may be supportive to you as progress in your healing or awakening journey.

The first is my **Break Free to Brilliance Podcast,** where my guests share their experiences of breaking free, finding their genius—their gift of brilliance to share in the world and how they stood in their power.

You can find the weekly podcast episodes here:

https://anchor.fm/seema-giri

If you want to get more clarity, support, and accountability as you navigate to your **new "normal,"** I offer several self-paced group workshops and personal coaching.

1. Group Coaching: **Break Free to Brilliance (16-week program)**
   For women entrepreneurs and leaders who feel burnt out, overwhelmed, and exhausted and want to live life to the fullest and reclaim their body, mind, and soul to live in the flow of their passion by building a strong wellness foundation.

2. Master Classes
   - Mastering Your Gut Health Workshop
   - 5-Day Thyroid Weight Loss Plan
   - Women's Hormones
   - Self Esteem/Self Love
   - Biohacking Your Life

3. Free Resources: As you navigate how you want to move forward, we are continuously coming up with new resources. You can find them at www.seemagiri.com. Here is a free gift to get you started: visit http://bit.ly/10WaysToBrilliance for a free gift on 10 Ways to Embrace Your Brilliance.

4. Healthy tools: Key catalysts in turning my health around are whole food supplements and the tower garden. You can find more information at www.seema.juiceplus.com or www.seemagiri.com.

If you are ready to shine and share your story on how you broke free from your challenges and are living life on your terms and if you are ready to help others stand in their power, you can participate in our upcoming anthologies and podcast.

If you would like to personally connect with me to explore some opportunities in my programs, podcasts, and book writing projects, schedule a time with me at http://bit.ly/TalkwithSeema, or you can email me at seema@seemgiri.com.

May you always *stand in your power*!

"There are two primary choices in life: to accept conditions as they exist, or accept the responsibility for changing them."
Dennis Waitley

What choices are you making?

www.ingramcontent.com/pod-product-compliance
Lightning Source LLC
LaVergne TN
LVHW020627100826
845148LV00012B/2081

* 9 7 8 1 7 3 5 0 2 5 5 0 6 *